From Success Came True Love

*Enemies and
Eventually Lovers*

J. D. Hova

J. D. HOVA PUBLISHING
JDH
WHERE IDEAS COME TO LIFE

TABLE OF CONTENTS

C H A P T E R   1

Twenty-seven-year-old Samantha stood before the large mirror in her lodge. The soft chiming of the clock gave a slow and steady rhythm to the cool Monday morning. Samantha breathed and smacked her lips; she knew how hectic Mondays were. She spared a glance at the wall clock; it was almost fifteen minutes before seven on the dot. By half past seven, she was sure to answer a query from her hypertensive boss and CEO. She picked up a brush and did a little retouch on her shoulder-length brunette hair. Her hazel eyes held beautiful sparks, and she blinked rapidly, fluttering her wavy eyebrows. She straightened the collar of her suit and walked towards the door. She heard the soft barks of her bulldog; she flashed a smile at the dog that wagged its tail in reply.

"See you in the evening," she said and unlocked the main door. She shut it, and she strutted her way to the garage where she parked her Benz. As she arrived at her parked car, she grabbed her sunglasses out of an elegant Louis Vuitton purse and put them on. She exuded boss vibes, and she loved the feeling. She unlocked the car and ignited the engine; the drive to the firm where she worked was a fifteen-minute journey. But as a fast driver, she was sure to arrive in less than ten minutes. She reached down for the stereo and inserted her favorite jam by Kendrick Lamar. His voice was the motivation she needed, and she always loved it.

In less than ten minutes, she pulled her vehicle into the parking lot of *Kings Consolidated.* She killed the engine and walked straight into the hallway; a lanky lady in a pink chiffon suit approached Samantha with a cup of coffee.

"Freshly brewed, just as you love it Miss," the lady rapped with a smile.

Samantha smiled back, "Thanks Georgina. Is Mr. Johnson on seat?"

"I don't think so."

Samantha took a deep breath of relief; at least she would escape his early morning scolding sessions. She smiled at Georgina, "That will be all."

"You look beautiful today, as always."

A pink sensation flushed through Samantha's cheeks, "Thank you Miss Georgina. I need to set somethings in place for the day's work."

Samantha walked past her, sipping the freshly brewed coffee. The adrenaline boost rushed through her veins, and the coffee was already pumping in her blood, giving her a strong boost for the day. As she stepped on the stairs that led to her office, she heard her name.

"Samantha."

The voice called again; she recognized the voice. It was her friend Rebecca Martinez. Samantha took a deep breath and retraced her steps back into the waiting arms of her friend. They hugged and then shook hands.

"Becky, I love your perfume," Samantha complimented.

"It was a gift from a friend. Remember the guy I told you about, he came all the way from Oklahoma to see me," Becky muttered excitedly.

"That's cool," Samantha replied. "I need to run a few checks on some document before Mr. Johnson arrives."

"Oh, the hardworking Sam. I am actually heading to the cafe for another cup of coffee" Becky smiled.

"You better be on seat before the Boss arrives, you won't want him having your head on a platter," Sam pointed.

"The Boss got nothing on me." She tilted her neck backward, and her wavy black hair spread to the sides. She smiled again, revealing a brilliant set of teeth.

Sam couldn't help but smile back at her, "I know you could smile all day. But we aren't doing a smiling competition."

Becky chuckled, "I see what you did there. Don't be a smart ass, you will end up puncturing your pride."

Sam blew her a kiss and headed to the stairs. She used her card and swiped, and the door unlocked with a beep. As she stepped in, the light flickered on, and the air conditioner came on with a wheezing sound.

She placed her bag at the end of the table and dragged her laptop closer. As she went to boot it, the landline rang. She wheeled herself to the table and reached for it.

Her heart skipped as she realized that it was the cold voice of Mr. Thomas Johnson, her Boss. He was exceptionally strict on Mondays, and Sam didn't want to be the object his frustration was directed to. She just wished all was well.

"Miss Williams, I need you in my office now."

The line went dead. Typical Mr. Johnson, he wasn't a man of many words. She got up, straightened her corporate skirt, and headed out of her office. She stepped into the elevator and pressed a button, it took her to the top floor, and she stepped out. She took a deep breath and headed towards Mr. Johnson's office. She barely rapped a knock, and the door was opened. She stepped into the cold office, and her eyes met with his own. He raised his gaze and stared into her eyes; his piercing blue eyes had this strong affluence and warmth, and she felt herself being carried away. As he cleared his throat, she fidgeted. His presence was imposing, and his face had a deep grimace.

"Sit," he said and pushed his tablet forward. He put the tip of his pen into his mouth and tilted forward.

"As you can see, Kings Consolidated has expanded operations across the states and we have new investors all the way from Asia stepping in."

Sam nodded; she couldn't afford to miss anything he was saying.

"In the next forty minutes, I would be having a meeting with some investors from Germany. They just arrived at the airport and I need to start making drafts for the presentations."

Sam's heart skipped, "Drafts?"

He stared at her with a skeptical look, "Yeah, drafts."

She chuckled bitterly and tried to maintain a calm composure, "You asked me to prepare the statistics record for auditing. And it was supposed to be a hundred-page draft. I am still on the twentieth page and I need to submit it this Friday. Adding this one to it is going to be a great load."

Mr. Johnson chuckled, "I don't pay you to lazy around, dress cute and drink my coffee. You are here to work your ass off."

"I beg to differ Sir; I won't be able to meet up on the both projects."

"Miss Williams, we are done here. I need everything by Friday this weekend," he said and reached for his tablet.

**

Samantha stepped out of the office with a deep scowl on her face. She tried to balance her weight on her stilettos, but it seemed she was going to fall anytime soon. The workload was just too much for her, and obviously, she was crashing under the weight. She had used make-up to mask the sleeping bags that formed under her eyelids.

She held the wall slowly and walked into the elevator. Her eyes began to turn as she realized that she was to turn in over three-hundred-page draft and presentation files by weekend. As the elevator reached the end point, she stepped out and dragged her leg towards her office. Her mind was far away from her body; she kept moving until she slammed into a body, and hot liquid spilled on her skin.

"Jesus fucking Christ!" Sam gasped and stepped back.

"Sam, what is it? Hope you were not burnt by my coffee?" Becky asked.

"No," Sam replied and reached for a small towel hanging by the side of a water dispenser. She wiped the remnant of the liquid and closed her eyes. Becky reached out to her and held her firmly.

"Are you alright, Sam?" She asked.

"Mr. Johnson wants me dead. Obviously, he knows no human is capable of pulling this feat. I am still not done with the statistics analysis of the company's sales. And now, he has given me another project. And you know how he takes deadlines seriously," Samantha complained.

Becky rubbed her shoulders, "What did he tell you to do this time?"

Sam shook her head, "Drafts, he wants me to prepare drafts for the presentations. And I am sure these drafts will be read during the board meeting on Friday. So, I am fucked."

"How far have you gone with the statistics?" Becky asked.

"The app I have been using for collation and documentation is messing up and making the work slow. And I'm just in the twentieth page and today is Monday. Becky, I am supposed to have a life aside this job," Sam complained.

"People are beginning to stare while you preach from the gospel of Lamentations. I will join you in the office soon. Let me clear this mess," Becky patted her shoulders and walked past her.

Sam took a deep breath, tilted her neck, and walked to her office. Her hazel eyes had lost their sparks, and her shoulders dropped. She swiped her card, stepped into the office, and slumped onto the chair. She pushed her laptop closer and wanted to type, but she ended up tapping the keys furiously, almost with the intention of damaging it. She heard a knock, and she tapped on the open button installed on the table. It was Becky again with her warm smile. She stepped in with two cups of coffee.

"Do you want to fuel your system with coffee?" Sam asked; there was something about Becky. She knew just how to light a room up with her infectious smile.

"Nothing beats the feeling of a freshly brewed coffee," Becky smiled and placed the cups on the table.

"Mr. Johnson is a bitch. That I know of," Sam muttered.

"Just smile, you are too pretty to keep a grimace," Becky stared into Sam's hazel eyes.

Sam couldn't help but smile, then dragged her laptop closer, "It's going to be a long day."

CHAPTER 2

Sam was curled on the sofa with her laptop in front of her. Her lacy nightie was lying peacefully at the foot of the chair. She was still collating figures for the board meeting, which was to happen in the next three hours.

Today was Friday, 3:00 am on the dot, and this week, she barely had enough sleep. She kept typing with almost bloodshot eyes, and after two hours passed, she was done. She breathed a sigh of relief and reached for her alarm on the footstool. She tweaked the alarm to 6:00 am and laid down to catch some sleep.

She felt a gentle muzzling on her arm, and her eyes popped open. Her pet dog was staring at her with what looked like pity in his eyes. Sam turned her gaze to the alarm clock. "Shit," she muttered and jumped off the sofa, almost throwing her laptop to the ground. She pulled off her nightie before she got into her room, and her chubby ass shook as she kept racing. Minutes later, she was done bathing, and she applied her body cream swiftly. She pulled off her shower cap and opened the drawers in which she placed her underwear. She wore them swiftly and decided to settle for a peach-colored peplum gown. She reached for her suede shoes and put them on. She stared at her face in the mirror, there was no time for makeup, but she was still pretty. She reached for her gold-plated wristwatch and peered at it; it was almost 8.

She rushed into her car without saying goodbye to her pet. She arrived at the firm at exactly 8:00 and parked her car behind Mr. Johnson's Bentley. She picked up her laptop and rushed towards the boardroom. Her heart kept beating wildly as she placed her hand on the knob. She pushed it open, and she breathed a sigh of relief. The meeting hadn't yet begun. She walked towards the wing Becky sat.

"You are late," Becky pointed with a smile.

Sam rolled her eyes, "Don't go there. In the past five days, I have barely had up to four hours sleep."

"You are hardworking and I admire that. Maybe that's why your Boss wants to work your ass off. He needs you to build this company."

Sam shrugged, "He wants me dead. This weekend, I need to try as much as getting enough sleep."

"That has always been your schedule. Work hard during the week days, sleep during weekends. You rarely go for outings," Becky said.

"Becky, I need to rest. Do you want me dead because of Insomnia?" She asked.

"Talk about the devil," Becky raised her gaze upwards.

Samantha followed the direction of her eyes and saw Mr. Johnson. He was in a top to neck pullover which clung to his well-chiseled body. He had a glass on his face, which made him look nerdy and sexy. But the stern aura still hovered around him. He walked over to his seat with a few members of the board. The hall was dead quiet. His personal secretary got up and read the proceedings of the meeting. Thirty minutes into the meeting, Samantha Williams was called to present the statistics for the company's investment.

She got up with a laptop, and Becky gave her a reassuring smile. She connected the laptop to the projector, and it displayed figures on the screen. She took a deep breath and started explaining. From the corner of her eyes, she could see the disapproving glances of Mr. Johnson.

"Miss Williams, I beg to interrupt," Mr Johnson said.

Sam rolled her eyes, *Son of a bitch!*

"Any problem, Sir?" She asked.

"I don't know if you take the board for fools, or maybe you think everyone here are so daft not to see through your folly."

"Jesus Christ," Sam couldn't help but mutter.

"Your figures aren't verified. If we were to be in the world trade fair meeting, is this what you will present?" There was a glow of anger in his eyes.

Sam's buried her face as the embarrassment got to her; she lifted her face and stared at her Boss squarely, "Everything here is what I got from the various department."

Mr. Johnson chuckled, "What a fucking excuse. A fucking stupid excuse. Pardon my language but this shit is just suffocating me. You had a whole week to review your numbers and ask questions. The departmental heads were here; you couldn't ask why the stock numbers are decreasing."

Sam chuckled, "I had barely a week to work on a hundred-page presentation. Still in the same week, I still had this to submit. The processing app has been crashing during usage and I had to do most of the collation manually. Where is the time to go round asking questions? I denied myself sleep…"

"Shut up," Mr. Johnson slammed his fist on the table, causing Sam to jerk. "There is no excuse for incompetence. You, Samantha Williams, you are one of the top shots in this company. But yet, you keep messing up. You need to go back and get the figures straight."

Sam smiled bitterly; her eyes were bloodshot and red. Why does Johnson not see all her efforts? For the past four years, she had sacrificed her comfort to ensure her duties were discharged properly. Why does he like capitalizing on a single mistake which wasn't hers? She only worked with the figures she was given.

"Miss Williams, I am disappointed in you. Before you present things like this, you need to make sure you get your facts straight. I won't blame the HOD. The blame is on you," Mr. Johnson said. "Gross Incompetence."

Sam swallowed, and she felt the sting of hot tears; she didn't want to give Mr. Johnson the satisfaction of seeing her tears. She placed the laptop on the table, moved over to her seat, grabbed her bag, and left the boardroom. She had never felt such humiliation in her life.

**

"You can't do this," Becky followed Sam as she walked towards the elevator.

Sam turned abruptly to her, "I want to give him a piece of my mind."

Becky stood before her, "I think that's a bad idea."

"Becky, you know how I have laboured for this company. The sleepless night, the stress, the pains. Only to be humiliated in such manner."

Becky breathed in tiredly, "You know that's how Mr. Johnson behaves."

"I am not taking it again," she said and stepped into the elevator. Sam was shivering as the elevator chimed and went up. As the elevator landed, she stepped out of it and headed to Mr. Johnson's office. She didn't even knock; she pushed the door open and stepped in.

Mr. Johnson was having a meeting with a few investors; he looked up and saw Sam fuming, her nostrils widened. The ethereal beauty was replaced with a dark scowl of fury.

"Excuse me gentlemen," he said and walked out of the office. He signaled for Sam to meet him in the corridor. Sam stepped out and slammed the shut.

"You are cruel, selfish and condescending. You know all the effort I have put into this company. The sleepless nights, look at my eyes. I haven't had a good sleep routine. And after my efforts, you stand there and open your damn mouth to talk thrash at me in the board room."

"Miss Williams…."

"You are the definition of a loser. And I can't keep working for a vicious creature who cannot appreciate a valuable treasure. I put it to you Mr. Thomas Johnson that I am a class of my own. Now, cross examine this; you gave me less than a week to turn in a hundred pages' project, you still gave me presentation drafts to work on. I delivered, no mortal can do that in three weeks. But I did it in less and instead of you to castigate your HOD, you brought the blame on me. You are fucking insensitive," Samantha roared.

Mr. Johnson was shocked; he just stared on.

"I quit," she said and walked out on him.

Sam stepped out of the elevator to meet Becky, pacing around. As she saw Becky, she almost broke into tears. But she kept her eyes wide open to prevent the tears from falling. Becky stared at her face; she knew the worst had happened.

Sam nodded at her and sniffed, Becky opened her arms, and Sam ran in for a hug.

"It's his loss baby," Becky whispered.

"I need to leave," Sam said.

"I really don't have anything to do today. All my reports have been submitted, I will join you," Becky said and rushed to get her bag.

Sam moved into her car and closed her eyes in a bid to control her emotions; she didn't regret her actions. Rather, she felt relieved and happy. As Becky stepped into the car, Sam ignited the engine.

"Are you in the right frame to drive?" Becky asked.

Sam nodded, "Sure, I am fine."

"Sure?" Becky raised an eyebrow.

"Sure," Sam replied.

"Did you call him a son of a bitch?" Becky asked.

"I don't need to call him that. I have this strong feeling that he knows his identity," Sam replied. "But what I told him, God knows I have been meaning to say it for quite a long time."

CHAPTER 3

Sam groaned in relief as she stepped out of her bed. She had slept for roughly eight hours, and she felt refreshed. She looked at the table clock lying by her side; it was almost dusk. A familiar scent hit her nose, and a smile spread on her face. She knew it was Becky's pies. Those pies were the best pies she ever tasted, and she missed them. She swung her feet off the bed and moved into the kitchen. Becky was in a kitchen apron while she threw some debris in the trash can.

"I almost thought you were dead?" Becky taunted.

"Huh?" Sam raised an eyebrow; she picked up a pie and munched it. Her taste buds juggled in excitement as the rich taste of the pie played around her tongue.

"You slept for hours. Girl, you really needed it," Becky smiled soothingly.

"Thanks for sticking by," Sam said and grabbed the tray that contained the pies.

Becky chuckled, "I figured out that I haven't had time to display my culinary skills. I decided to make use of it today. I might not be going back to that work again."

Sam turned to her, "You can't quit because I did."

Becky sank her ass on the chair, "You are the reason I always put my heart and soul to work. You are the reason I came to Kings Consolidated in the first place. You are like my whole inspiration and now, you quit. What's the point? Don't worry about me, I will go back to my mum's canteen and prepare some delicious puddings."

Sam smiled, "I miss those puddings."

"Worry less, you will miss them no more. So, what's the way forward?"

Sam crossed her legs and took a deep breath, "I had this thought on my mind since the beginning of the month."

"What thought?" Becky asked.

Sam rubbed her palms together, "I want to start up my own firm."

Becky shifted backward and stared at her friend, "Are you sure you are ready for this?"

"I have never been this sure in my life. Look, I have a few contacts of some investors. You remember Jason, the Greek guy? I could use his connections to pierce through the stock market. Once the numbers are promising, we have a lot of investors. Then we invest in real estates. Get some undeveloped land and develop it," Sam rapped.

Becky folded her arms, "That means I won't go back to my mum's canteen right?"

"It's your choice. But I will need your help more than ever," Sam whispered.

"You will always have my help," Becky smiled.

Becky stood up, "But when the news gets to Mr. Johnson, he will see you as a competition. He might accuse you of…"

Sam rolled her eyes, "The sky is large for every bird to fly."

Becky nodded, "I believe in you and I know that you are strong, bold, intelligent and hardworking."

Sam smiled, "Thanks Becky."

After munching the pies and watching their favorite soap opera, Sam reached for her laptop. She decided to search for some underdeveloped properties in Texas. She sent an email to Jason Stone, her friend who owned one of the biggest estates in Texas. She also decided to reach out to other cities across the states. She sent emails to a few of the investors she had close contact with. After about three hours, she decided to go for a walk with Becky and her pet.

As they strolled under the moonlight, Sam's phone beeped. She pulled it out of her pocket and stared at the screen. It was an email from an estate agency. They were having a ted-fun event in the next three days.

"I just got an invite to attend a ted fun event from Kriss agency," Sam said and pocketed her phone.

"You going?" Becky asked.

"Sure," Sam nodded, "I need all the help and mentor ship I can get. And the event is basically for CEO and entrepreneurs."

They strolled for about an hour before Sam escorted Becky to the park. Minutes later, Sam returned home. She went into the bathroom for a bath; this time, the water was therapeutic because it washed off the stress away. Now, she felt free and happy. She was sure that if she lasted till the workday was over, Mr. Johnson was sure to bombard her with projects and endless demands of work, drafts, and countless presentations. She never had a weekend for herself. As she stepped out of the bathtub, she walked nude to the bed and picked up a towel. She dried herself and strapped her nightie on. She picked up her phone and decided to do something she hadn't done for a long time.

She logged into her Tinder account. She was greeted by pictures of handsome men, and she realized how much she had lost her fun life working at Kings Consolidated. It has been years since she had a pleasurable outing, and she craved one. She searched through the profiles, and a particularly handsome man caught her fancy. She slid into his inbox and dropped a message. He was online, and they started chatting. She learns he was a lecturer who worked in a research institution in Saint Albany and came to Texas to spend his vacation. They talked into the night, and Sam found herself laughing to his witty replies. She realized the dude was intelligent and had a strong sense of humor. Sam got up, went into the kitchen, and grabbed a bottle of wine before returning to the room to continue the conversation.

They chatted till midnight, and they fixed a meeting for the next evening. Sam wasn't feeling sleepy, she decided to visit Netflix. She had missed a couple of her favorite movies in the last couple of months. She watched three series of her favorite anime and ended up sleeping at dawn. Hours later, she woke up at exactly midday and decided to do some chores. As she remembered she had a date later in the evening, a smile lit up on her face.

**

Sam combed her hair for the umpteenth time and stared at the mirror. She was some minutes late for the date, and she had a hard time choosing what to wear. She found out that in the past years, she did more of buying cooperate wears than dinner gowns. She had to settle for an off-shoulder split thigh sequin gown. It was a birthday gift three years ago. She grabbed her purse and her phone and stepped out. Her pet dog wriggled its tail towards her while she waved at him.

She got into the car and sped off to the location. It was an exquisite bar in the middle of the city with a fancy rooftop. She killed the engine and stepped onto the rooftop. There she saw him, his blue eyes seizing her up. That was the same face she saw on Tinder; he looked more handsome in reality than in the pictures.

The man stood up with a charming smile lurking around his lips, "Samantha?"

Sam walked closer, trying to remember his name, "You didn't tell me your name?"

He smiled fully, revealing a gaped dentition, "I am Kelvin. You didn't care to ask".

Her eyes rolled in their sockets, "Thank you Kelvin. I am sorry to keeping you waiting."

"I would wait for eternity, if that means waiting for a pretty girl like you," he said.

Sam felt the heat flush through her cheeks; she walked slowly and sat on the chair.

Kelvin ordered a smoothie and a sandwich. They ate together in silence.

"So, you told me that you just resigned from your job?" He asked.

Sam nodded, "I did. And I am looking at starting my own firm."

"That's good. So, you have never dated before?" He asked.

Sam nodded, "Since after my time in the university, I haven't. Work took all my time."

"I see. Such work is toxic."

Sam nodded, "Damn toxic. So, tell me about your love life?"

Kelvin chuckled, "Nothing really exciting about my love life. I am married to a lady that I don't love."

On hearing the word *marriage,* every attraction she had for him was watered down. She chuckled and sipped from her smoothie, "Why so?"

"I thought I married a human being. She just changed all of a sudden and became this toxic soul. I had to run away from Saint Albany to clear my head."

Sam smiled, "That means we both ran away from something."

Kelvin nodded, and they laughed. His gaze lingered on her face, and Sam avoided those blue eyes.

"You are pretty, Sam. I see strength all over you. I would have loved to get to know you better but my time here is almost at hand."

"Yeah, you need to see how you can work things out between you and your wife," Sam said with a raised brow.

Kelvin called the waitress and ordered some chicken strips. It was brought, and Sam took the first bite.

"I have a friend that makes things like this. Hers is actually more delicious," Sam said.

"Is that friend as pretty as you?" Kelvin asked with a wink.

Sam chuckled and shrugged, "I don't know. But she is pretty too."

The two of them discussed all through the evening until Sam had to leave. Kelvin was going to head to the airport the next day. They hugged briefly and parted ways with a promise to always keep in contact.

Samantha Williams regarded her face in the steaming mirror. Not bad, considering that she had been up half the night going through some research topic sent to her by her investor friend, Jason.

"I want to start this company," She thought fiercely.

Today was the Ted fun event, and she needed to be at the grounds early enough. She settled for a polka-dotted gown and a scarf around her brunette hair. She picked the file that contained the research she did and a few investors email. She was going to send them some vital information later in the day. She picked up her car key and made a mental note to buy lunch after the event. She wasn't someone who loved cooking. The event was to be held at the central mall, which was a fifteen minutes' drive from where she stayed. She arrived and made some registration with the protocol officer at the gate. She displayed her invite, and she was allowed into the main hall. As she pushed the door open, her face widened into a smile. The hall was calm, with people numbering up to a hundred sitting. There was a huge projector displaying a jingle about the benefits of micro-investment and the future of investors in the state. Sam moved to the third row as directed by a protocol officer and sat down. She placed her files on a small slab beside her and fixed her gaze on the projector.

"Hey."

Sam turned to see a man by her side; from his gaze and accent, Sam knew he was Asian.

"Hey," Sam replied.

He took a deep breath and stretched his hands, "I am Marcus Chen."

She smiled and reciprocated the gesture, "I am Samantha Williams."

The sound of the microphone came up, and the host, clad in an all-white suit, mounted the stage. Some dignitaries were recognized, and even the State's trade fair chairman was in attendance. Top businessmen, CEO(s), and entrepreneurs were called to speak, and Sam took note of the important nuggets and information.

"Since cryptocurrency and other digital assets has swept over the business facet of the world's market. Mr. Marcus Chen will teach us how we can access these assets to our own use. Marcus Chen owns one of the largest digital crypto mining firms and also a major shareholder in Gemsbok group of companies."

Sam stared in surprise as Marcus stood up and walked briskly to the stage. She wondered why he didn't sit with other speakers at the podium. He looked rather too humbled and smart. She listened to him and made a mental note to ask him some vital questions after the event. From what she gathered, she had a concrete plan to bring investors into her project and made sure they had at least sixty percent of their RIO. That was going to be a big risk, but she was willing to take it. With high-profit returns, her investors were sure to stick around.

Three hours later, the meeting ended. Though Marcus didn't return to his seat anymore, she had to go meet him. She straightened her gown, grabbed her files, and headed to the podium, but she was restrained. She decided to wave at him; he saw her gesture and beckoned on her. He signaled to the protocol officer to let her pass.

Sam moved with boldness, this time with a smile on her face. "You were the best speaker."

He smiled. "Thanks Miss Williams."

"I have a few questions for you, if you don't mind."

He rubbed his palms together, "Maybe you could ask me these questions while we take lunch?"

"Lunch?" Her face lit up, this was a life time opportunity, she thought.

Marcus spoke with a few of the speakers and then stepped out of the podium. Sam offered to hold his case, but he refused with a smile.

"I have a guard and I don't want to stress a pretty lady," He flashed a funny smile.

She saw his car; it was the latest Rolls-Royce edition. "I came with mine."

"My guard will drive it," He replied, "Come on."

She threw her key to the macho guard and stepped into the vehicle. The interior of the car reeked of wealth. There was a silver-colored chandelier on the roof and a small pocket freezer by the side.

"I am honored, Mr. Chen," She said with a smile.

"Yeah, first time you stepped in, I felt this strong sharp energy from you. And I knew you were a woman of purpose. And I love women with such keen aura."

Sam nodded thoughtfully, "Thank you."

The car pulled over in front of a Chinese restaurant. They stepped out, and Marcus pulled off his jacket and ran his hands into his curly hair.

"I have another speaking engagement at San Antonio," He said.

Sam nodded, "Sorry, I won't take too much of your time."

"Don't worry; I have three hours before I leave."

They went into the restaurant, and he ordered a dish of Peking duck served with pancakes and vegetables.

Sam stared at the menu, her eyes roamed through in confusion. Marcus noticed it, "You haven't tried a Chinese dish before?"

Sam smiled, "I have."

"Try congee. It is rice porridge and it is delicious," He suggested.

Sam released a breath, "Rice porridge it is."

They ate lunch in silence, and she was surprised that it actually tasted great; she loved the sliced pork and the scallions. Chinese dishes weren't as bad as Becky painted them to be. Sam noticed Marcus was a very slow eater; he took his time to bite stuff. Maybe he had all the time in the world, she shrugged.

"You know before I came to the states, I worked in my granddad's kitchen in China. I cooked for five years until I realized that cooking wasn't for me. But there was an incident, actually. A fire outbreak, someone wanted me out of the property. That was the push I needed to leave that terrain."

Sam nodded, "Was anyone hurt during the fire outbreak?"

"Just a friend, he suffered third degree burns. But of recent, I made him go through one of the best cosmetic surgeries."

"That's good," She replied.

"Back then in China, those days were the worst days," He leaned back on the chair.

**

"You had questions for me huh?" He reached for the serviette and wiped his mouth.

"Yeah," Samantha breathed, "I am actually looking at starting my own firm. I was looking at starting up some real estate projects and then building a portfolio for investors to step in. I have some written drafts for the business." She shifted the file to Marcus.

"I am not with my glasses," He said.

He pulled out his phone and dialed his guard's number. The man returned shortly with his glasses. Marcus put it on and stared at the paper critically. A smile formed on his face, and he nodded.

"You have a good business plan, but it isn't enough to bring in the kind of investors you need." He removed his glasses and placed it inside the case. "Before investors part with their money, they must ensure that the business plan is feasible and grounded. Your plan needs visible goals and your goals must also bring tangible result to the table. They need to see plans that can bring profitability."

Sam nodded, "I was thinking…"

"I sincerely know what you are thinking of. You think the ROI will attract investors? Yes, it will but the question is, at what cost? You will be running down the gross capital because it isn't strong enough to churn out such return of investment."

"So, the plan won't work?" She asked.

"The entire plan won't. But, we can build on the ideas, draft a better and more specific goal oriented idea."

"Master, teach me," She said and bowed.

Marcus smiled, "What areas do you have in mind for the real estate development?"

Sam tilted forward, "A Greek friend of mine brought some suggestions, and I did a great deal of research. Texas is rich in landed properties with value in tens of million. I was looking at the Chihuahua desert. With the right development, the place could spring up. And moreover, it is close to the national park."

Marcus clapped his hands, "You are bright. I never thought you could figure out such. I would want you to attend the summit with me this evening. It's strictly on invitation but you would get to meet more bright minds and top business men. I would pitch your idea with them on a more polished note while you do some homework on your investment plan."

She nodded, "That's a fair deal. Thank you, Mr. Chen; I am so honored to sit at the same table with you."

"I love to relate with powerful minds, people that can take the business world by storm."

"Can I ask for a favor?" She asked.

Marcus raised an eyebrow, "Okay?"

"I need you to be my mentor. Not like I want to be a burden, but I just need your insightful opinion until I stand on my feet."

He took a deep breath, "That's okay. Something just crossed my mind, you can actually connect with a few manufacturing industries. I will link you with them; you could have supplies of tech devices. The rare ones and probably make supplies to the consumers."

She nodded, "Thank you very much Mr. Marcus."

"It is almost time for my next event."

CHAPTER 5

Samantha groaned in relief as she killed the engine. She was greeted by the barking of her pet dog. Her legs were sore, and she immediately pulled off her shoe before stepping out of the car. As she moved to the door, she noticed a soft music playing from the sitting room. Someone was definitely inside the house. She pushed the door open and was surprised to see Becky setting up the dining for dinner.

"Hey, you never told me you were coming?" Sam asked in surprise.

Becky held her waist in askance, "I called you countless times."

Sam raised an eyebrow; she reached for her purse and took out her phone. She then remembered that she muted it. She could see eighteen missed call notifications, specifically from Becky.

"I am sorry. Today was damn stressful but also productive," Sam lowered herself into the chair.

Becky retrieved a pack of yogurt from the freezer, "The ted fun event took that long?"

Sam shook her head in negative, "Not that. I actually met this Marcus Chen."

Becky's eyes brightened, "You met Marcus Chen?"

"You know him?" Sam asked.

Becky nodded, "He owns Gemsbok."

Sam nodded, "He was actually the speaker at the first event. We met, connected and had lunch. He went through my business plan and gave me some tips. Then he invited me to another submit and I got to meet some millionaires. Right now, I have a vision for my company, I just need to make some changes to the blueprint and also prepare a proposal."

Becky got up and caressed her shoulders, "I am proud of you."

"How was your day?" Sam asked.

Becky shrugged, "I did some online deliveries for old clients. Apparently, they want me cooking again."

"So, what's your plan?" Sam asked.

"I want to help you build this company. You deserve it."

Sam nodded with a smile, "Thank you."

"Come have some dinner. I made puddings and turkey stew," Becky offered.

Sam got up with a groan, "You know, I tried a Chinese dish today."

"Yuck," Becky's face screwed up in disgust.

"It was delicious," Sam shrugged, "You should try it."

"Nah, I will pass," Becky said and pulled a chair for Sam.

"You will make a good PA," Sam joked.

"No. I will rather make a good CEO," Becky chided.

They sat for dinner and ate while Becky kept talking about a lot of things. Sam was a good listener, and they spent over an hour talking.

"I hope you are going to crash for the night?" Sam asked.

"Isn't that obvious?" Becky asked.

"I hope you're not also in a hurry to leave tomorrow?" Sam asked.

"Need me for something?" Becky asked.

"I just need to go through some intricate details on my business plan. I need your ideas too."

Becky nodded, "Sure, you have it."

Sam wished her a goodnight and headed for her room. It was a relief to shed her clothes, and she stood nude in the center of the room. She moved into the bathroom and turned on the tap to the shower. The warm water cascaded over her, and she leaned over and turned the knob to fill the bathtub. In hopes to relax she lowered herself in the tub, leaned back submersed her naked body in the warm water resting the back of her head on the cooler porcelain on the back edge of the tub. The thought of her firm was still on her mind as she spilled the liquid lather over her body. Thirty minutes later, she was out. She slid into her nightie and moved to the sitting room to get her file. She was surprised to see Becky in front of the television.

"Aren't you sleeping?" Sam asked.

Becky shrugged, "You actually need to sleep."

"I just want to pack my bag," Sam said.

"No, no. I don't want you breaking down because of lack of sleep," Becky said.

"I just want …"

"Once you get hold of that file, you might spend the whole night working on it. Go to bed, get refreshed, we work tomorrow," Becky said.

Sam smiled, "You scold exactly like my mum."

"You work too hard, Sam. Go to bed," Becky pointed in the direction of the room.

Sam took a deep breath and turned to her room. She switched off the light and jumped on the soft bed. She moaned as she pulled the blanket over her warm skin. She felt the storm and knew it was going to rain. She closed her eyes and muttered a few words of prayers.

*

Sam came awake with the start at the sound of her alarm. She blinked until the glowing screen of the clock swam into focus: 5:35. She remembered she had no work to do and wanted to lay back down. But then, she remembered her business plan. She swung her foot off the bed and walked to the sitting room. The television was on and muted, and Becky dozed off in the chair. Her soft snores filter through the calm air in the sitting room. That was her habit, sleeping while watching television. Sam picked up her bag and headed back to her room. She switched on the light and spread the drafts she prepared. She picked up her laptop and googled up the locations of the places that needed development. She had ten places on her mind, but she needed to narrow it down to five for now. She picked up her proposal memo and studied it. From there, she drafted an email and sent it to the private e email of the tech company she needed to partner with.

She already spoke with a few potential investors, and she browsed through their feedback. She had scripted every report in a separate draft. She noticed the similarities and differences in their feedback. She included it in her proposal and read through it again. She wondered if she would change the ROI. The ROI was the return on investment for each investor. She wasn't yet certain of the amount of money she would use as the capital. But, she was sure that her plans were becoming feasible. Her phone beeped, and it was a reply from the tech company. She read through the email, and she knew she had to double her plans to raise the funds that were needed.

**

As Sam was making some calculations, she raised her gaze up and saw the door move slowly. It was Becky; she kept yawning and blinking her eyes rapidly.

"Hey," Samantha said.

Becky sniffed, "I knew you would be up already. Last night episode of the *Garden* was terribly boring. I couldn't help but doze off."

Samantha nodded, "That has always been your excuse."

Becky sat on the bed, "So, what's up?"

Sam chuckled and took a deep breath; frustration was visibly written on her face.

Becky held her hands, "Hey, don't get yourself worked up. We will figure this out."

"I have the proposal mapped out. And the tech company which I am supposed to partner with are demanding a million dollar. I have just half of it."

Becky nodded thoughtfully, "How about the investors?"

Sam put the tip of her fountain pen in her mouth, "We can't get anything from the investors now. I still have a few registrations and some legal backing."

"I can squeeze out five thousand dollars for that. When are you going to start the process?"

Sam thought for a while, "This week."

Becky nodded, "I will make a transfer to you later in the day."

Sam sniffed, "Thanks Becky."

"And what's next?" Becky asked.

"I am going to call Jason later in the day. He is going to help me secure a building. Somewhere I can call the company's official building."

Becky smiled, "My girl is getting there."

Sam glared at her, "We aren't there yet."

Becky smiled, "Baby steps, baby steps my friend."

Sam relaxed her head on the bed rest, "I just hope this works out well."

Becky nodded, "It will. You are a strong lady and I know you can make it happen."

Sam reached out and held Becky's hands; she looked into Becky's eyes. Those eyes were soothing. Becky smiled, and Sam smiled too.

"You have been a true friend," Sam said.

"You earned it," Becky got up and left the room.

Sam reached for her phone and dialed Jason's number. She requested that he should search for a building, and she gave him her budget. She knew Jason would secure the best for her. The day was starting to break, and she had to be at the places she listed early enough to run some surveys. She slipped on a shirt and neatly tucked it into her combat trousers. She grabbed her car key, credit card, and headed out the door.

"Becky, I need to check out those areas before I draw my estimate," She said to Becky, who was busy in the kitchen.

"When will you be back?"

Sam shrugged, "I don't know yet. But I will keep you posted."

"Stay safe."

Sam stepped into her car and ignited the engine. She dialed the number of the evaluator and waited for it to ring.

"I am headed for the first site."

As she ended the call, Jason's call came in. Her eyes widened as she heard the news. In less than an hour, Jason had secured a building in the heart of San Antonio. She knew she had to check it out before the day was over.

CHAPTER 6

It's been two weeks and four days; *Williams Ventures* has officially been launched. Samantha was able to buy the building and also secure some landed properties. But now, the legal fees and other procurement had consumed a bulk of her cash, and she had fewer funds to procure the tech devices. She sat on a swivel chair and spun slowly, the tip of the fountain pen in her mouth. She glanced at her office again; she had taken time to redesign the office to give it a first-class outlook. The look that would attract investors to the company; She just employed a secretary while Becky was in charge of a few logistics and public running. She heard a knock, and she got up and arranged her skirt. She had been expecting a few investors that morning. The door was opened, and two men walked briskly into the office.

"Morning Gentlemen," Sam greeted with a light smile. She really hoped for something positive.

The men sat on the swivel chair, and the leader tilted forward, "Miss Williams, we received your email, but right now, we would need to get concrete information from you."

Sam nodded and took in an air of confidence, "Okay. Williams Ventures is a firm that will thrive well with the right partnership. We have assets in lands and we are now looking at venturing into tech. Since diversification is the key to financial power, I have been drawn to the notice of a body detoxifier which is a ninth generation tech device. I have the prototype already and we need to procure as our own invention."

One of the men nodded, and Sam took that as a cue that her proposal would be accepted.

"The complete prototype and rights to the tech product will cost a million dollar. We can start with half a million and trust me, in six months, your ROI will be double from your investment," Sam said, studying their faces.

"So, if we put in five hundred thousand dollars, we have a million dollars in half a year?" The man asked.

Sam nodded, "You will."

"Can I see what the tech device looks like?" One of the men asked.

Sam nodded and clicked on a folder on her laptop, she pushed it forward, and the men stared at it.

"With time, your ROI will be increased in a shorter duration. But now, we need to pierce the tech market," Sam said.

The man straightened the collar of his jacket, "Your proposal is enticing. But I must rather say that we are not going to be interested in investing."

Sam's heart skipped a bit, "May I ask why?"

"Your company is relatively new and you sound like an overconfident rookie. We have been in this business long enough to understand that you will go into financial crisis soon enough."

"Sir, you need to trust the system."

"Your tech device might not penetrate as far as you think it would. People are bit paranoid when it comes to using stuffs like that."

"Sir, once the benefit..."

"No, Miss Williams, this has been a complete waste of time. But if we consider your proposal, we will get back to you."

"I hope so," Sam smiled; she tried to keep the smile on as the men filed out of the office. Soon as the last man left, she rammed her fist into the table.

"Fuck," She pulled out her laptop and brushed through her schedule. Her face lightened as three notifications popped up. Two sets of investors promised to visit her firm before midday.

"Take a deep breath, you will be fine," She whispered to herself.

Two hours later, Sam heard a knock on her door. She lifted her gaze from the system to the door.

"Ma'am, a few investors want to see you."

She nodded and took a deep breath, *this must work out, and it has to.*

"A pleasant morning, lady and gentleman."

"A bright day, it is," The lady replied.

Sam narrated the proposal. "Trust me, this tech device has prospects. We are looking at making sure that every city in this country get access to it. And your initial investment will be doubled after six months."

"I don't invest in tech. I probably would do agriculture because it is more promising than tech," The lady said.

Jesus fucking Christ! Sam gasped, "Are we seriously comparing tech and agriculture here?"

"Perhaps if you can develop a device that can increase soil fertility, and crop productivity. I would invest. Right now, times are hard and dollars are hard to earn. I am sorry."

"Ma'am, this is a prospective billion-dollar investment."

"Miss Williams, your proposals sounding juicy, when I read it. But, judging from your vocal implementation, I can't risk it."

Sam breathed tiredly, "No problem ma'am, have a good day."

As they left, tears streamed down Sam's eyes. "This is bullshit."

She kept biting her nails nervously while staring at the laptop screen. One more meeting was left; she made the sign of the cross. She needed approximately half a million to procure the tech devices, then proceeds from it would be used for the estate development. She had her plans well mapped out, but the investors were disappointed.

An hour later, there was a knock on the door. Three men with deep scowl on their faces entered. Sam knew it might take a hard time convincing them, but she was ready. She wouldn't let the day end on a negative note. She needed to secure the funds before the week ran out, and she was running short of potential investors.

"Hello Gentlemen, welcome to *Williams Ventures.*"

The men listened with rapt attention as she presented her proposal.

"Do you have a team to ensure the marketing process goes well?"

Sam nodded, "I have set up a six-man team. But, the bulk of the marketing process will be done on the media. I strongly believe that once people see the result, they will want to get the product."

"I trust a product as this will be pretty expensive. What's your plan for the common people?"

"Health is wealth, and life is priceless," Sam said.

"We will get back to you," They said and got up.

**

"We will get back to you," The tall man said.

Sam knew that statement was a more sympathetic way of saying, 'not interested'. As the men left the office, she pushed her laptop aside and sobbed. Today was Friday, and one week had gone already with no hope for operation. She cracked her knuckles and rested her head on the table. She was beginning to feel a throbbing headache, and her eyes were hurting because of long hours of staring at the screen. The door to the office was unlocked, and Becky walked in and sat facing Sam.

"No good thing comes easy. I remember as a little girl, when my aunt started her bakery. She will sit for days with no customer in sight. But then, things started to pick up."

Sam raised her head, "We don't have time and I don't want to be tempted to sell off the landed properties."

Becky nodded, "I understand. I have watched you work so hard and I have also seen you achieve everything you ever wanted. This isn't an exception. Maybe you should call Marcus and see how he can help."

Sam nodded; she reached for her phone and scrolled through. "I don't have his private contact. I hope he answers this."

The phone rang for a while.

"You are onto the Personal Assistant of..."

"I want to speak with Mr. Marcus Chen, tell him that it is important. Please."

"And who are you?"

"Miss Williams, Samantha Williams."

There was a brief pause and then a familiar cough, "Miss Williams, so good to hear from you."

"Sir, I am near my breaking point," She whimpered.

"Business stress."

"I can handle the stress. Thing is, I have not been able to secure funds for my business. The investors are not promising either," Sam said.

Marcus thought for a while, "What about getting a loan?"

Sam nodded in negative, "I don't want a loan."

"New business owners run from loans."

"What I mean is, the bank won't give the required amount I need," Sam said.

"Visit the bank by Monday. Get what will be required to procure what you need for a small amount of people. Set up a team and start aggressive marketing. Let the product be less and the demands high. Try that and see."

"I will do that," Sam replied.

"Let us see how that performs the magic. You don't have to consider giving up, okay?" He said.

"Thank you Sir," She replied, and the call ended.

Sam's face lit up, "We will need a loan and a team."

Becky nodded, "We will need to employ right?"

Sam nodded in negative, "We aren't employing anyone. I need people who can give me result. I need some badasses in the marketing industry."

"You have someone in mind?" Becky asked.

Sam leaned back, "We will need to pay our old co workers a visit."

"What old co workers?" Becky asked.

"I know friends in Kings Consolidated that can give the result I need."

"You want to hijack co workers from your former Boss?" Becky raised her eyebrow.

Sam shrugged, "I have no choice."

CHAPTER 7

Sam combed her hair and smiled at the mirror. She took a deep breath and tried to summon her confidence. She knew she had to look confident to be able to convince her former co workers. The Monday evening was chilly, and she felt it was going to rain. She picked up her car key and her phone, stepping outside, she dialed Becky's number. Fifteen minutes later, Becky arrived. She took a deep breath and folded her hands.

"You are late," Sam glared.

"Sorry, I had a few stuffs to take care of," Becky replied.

They both stepped into the vehicle, and Sam engaged the gear. She turned the steering wheel furiously and drove into the expressway.

"I was able to secure the loan and I have sent the money to the tech company," Sam broke the silence.

"That's cool. So, whose house are you visiting first?" Becky asked.

"Tara Simmons," Sam replied.

Becky took a deep breath, "Sam, I still think you should consider employing new people."

Sam shook her head, "I need people whom I have trusted their efforts already."

She navigated through the busy street and sped into the next street.

"I hoped you did well to inform her?"

Sam nodded, "I did."

Sam killed the engine in front of a detached duplex. She stepped out of the car and walked through a dimly lit corridor. There was a fleet of stairs, and they climbed it until they arrived at a door.

Sam knocked on the door, and it was unlocked by a smiling lady with sharp green eyes.

"Tara," Sam called with a smile.

They hugged briefly. Tara turned and saw Becky, "Hi."

"Hi," Becky replied with a smile.

Tara tilted her neck, letting her shoulder-length blonde hair tilt to one side, "I missed you."

"I missed you too," Sam replied.

"Come in," Tara ushered them into her fairly furnished sitting room. "You know Mr. Johnson can't stop talking about you. He uses you as his reference point during meetings. He talks about how hardworking you were."

Becky scoffed, "The damage has already been done."

Tara sat down with a deep breath, "So, what brings you to my humble abode? You made me worried when you said that you wanted to see me."

Sam took a deep breath and flicked her hair, "I have started my own company. *Williams Ventures,* looking at delving into tech and real estate."

Tara clapped her hands in excitement, "I am proud of you. I have always admired your strength Miss Williams."

Sam tilted forward, "I need your help."

Tara squinted her eyes, "I am listening."

"For the number of years I have seen you work, I have always loved your intelligence and strategies. Right now, I am starting up a team to market a delicate tech product. The investment returns are high but we need to make sure we push this to the tech market."

Tara blinked, "I am listening."

"I am offering you a job in my firm," She said.

Tara gasped, "A job?"

Sam nodded, "I need you on my team."

Tara's hands shivered, "No offence intended, but I can't just leave Kings Consolidated. My future is there."

"Your future is guaranteed in my firm," Sam said.

"What is the pay grade?" Tara asked.

"We split the eventual profit while I pay back the bank and develop the properties I bought," Sam replied.

Tara leaned back on the chair, "This is too much for now. I have pending reports to file and I can't just leave."

Sam nodded, "I understand. But, I need you and that bright brain of yours."

Tara nodded, "I understand and I will love to work with you. But, you need to give me time please?"

Sam breathed, "Time is what we don't have now. Before the end of this month, we need to come up with a suitable plan. Trust me, you won't regret this move. I need you on my team and my team is the winning team."

Tara smiled, "I sincerely hope this act won't bring rivalry between you and Mr. Johnson. If he realizes this, he might…"

"Tara, I await your feedback," Sam pulled out her business card and handed it to her. "See you at work on Monday."

Tara nodded, "Okay Ma'am. I will try my best."

They exited the house, Becky and Sam ignited the engine, and they sped out of the house.

"I sincerely hope she buys the idea," Becky said.

Sam nodded, "She will. I trust her and our team will be better with her in it."

Becky nodded, "Anything else? I need to make some hot spaghetti sauce before hitting the bed."

"We still have one person we need to visit. And that will be done tomorrow," Sam said.

"Are we enlisting more people?" Becky raised her eyebrow.

"Just one last person," Sam said.

"Let me guess, Emily Thompson," Becky said.

Sam smiled, "Yeah, you got it right."

Becky raised a finger up, "I hope sincerely that this isn't a revenge plan?"

Sam chuckled, "Don't be petty. It is far from a revenge plan. We need a team."

"But you are going after the best hands in Kings Consolidated."

"Kings Consolidated has a lot of good hands. They won't miss a few," Sam said.

"A few, really?" Becky raised a brow.

"Becky, I only need two people. I don't need the whole company," Sam replied.

"I hope we are able to convince them," Becky said.

"Tara and Emily passed through my training. I taught them everything they had to know. So, they will see it as an honor working for me. I am not foolish to make this move on someone else," Sam answered.

"I can't wait to be your assistant. You owe me that promotion," Becky said.

"I am not promoting you. Why harbor such ideas?" Sam asked.

Becky shrugged, "I am the right person, okay? It is only natural that the baton comes to me."

"Oh, you are ridiculous," Sam said.

"I am looking at trying a new recipe tonight," Becky said thoughtfully.

Sam spared her a glance, "My kitchen is yours."

**

Becky couldn't make it this evening, so Sam had to go alone. She slid the key into the ignition and stepped on the gas pedal. Emily lived downtown with her fiancé and a kid. Thirty minutes later, Sam killed the engine in front of the building. She stepped out and saw Emily practicing with the guitar.

"Miss Williams," She gasped excitedly and rushed towards Sam.

"I'm glad you are well," Sam smiled at her.

"I saw your message that's why I stayed. I had fellowship tonight," Emily replied.

Sam nodded, "Sorry, I won't take too much of your time."

Emily led Sam inside and switched on the solar lamp, "What can I offer you?"

Sam nodded in negative, "Nothing. I am fine."

"Okay," Emily shrugged.

Sam took a deep breath and tilted forward, "You were one of the best interns I trained at Kings Consolidated. I need your help now."

Emily listened with rapt attention.

"I have launched my own company and I need a team to help publicize and market my tech device. I need a quick result that's why I want the best people on my team."

Emily chuckled, "You need me on your team?"

"I am offering you a job in my company," Sam replied.

Emily gasped, "That fast?"

Sam nodded, "Yeah. And I need you to start on Monday."

"Jesus Christ. I can't leave Kings Consolidated now."

Sam rolled her eyes, "In my company, every member of the team has direct access to shares from the profits."

Emily chuckled, "That means you want me to tender my resignation letter by the weekend?"

Sam nodded, "It's a move you won't regret, that I am sure of."

Emily took a deep breath, "Just wow."

Sam reached out and held her hands, "You don't have to fear anything. I would have simply employed new sets of people. But, now I need people with a proven track record. People like you."

Emily's face flushed, "Thanks for having confidence in me."

Sam nodded, "I trust you too well. And, I need you and that big brain of yours."

Emily nodded, "So, feel me on the company."

"The company for now is looking into real estate development and tech. There is a prototype up for sale and this device helps in detoxifying the body of harmful product. It is one of the best and I want to procure the device and register my trademark on it. Right now, the prototype and a couple of the devices have been secured."

Emily nodded, "That means you need a good marketing strategy right?"

Sam nodded, "Yeah, from there we could start attracting investors. The work will then be easier and it will speed up financing the estate development. I spent sleepless nights developing this plan; I just need the best strategy to implement it."

"Like you taught me, the best strategy comes from provocative thinking," Emily said.

"Thank you Emily, I hope to see you on Monday," Sam said.

Emily breathed thoughtfully, "Monday? Mr. Johnson will be pissed if I turn in incomplete templates this weekend."

"He will get another to do it. He hasn't cared about people's feelings before," Sam replied.

Emily nodded, "Let's see how it goes."

"I can count on you, Emily," Sam said, and they walked out together.

CHAPTER 8

Samantha got up from the bed as her alarm beeped. Today was Monday, and she dreaded the day. But today, she felt a tinge of fear and excitement. She wondered if Tara and Emily could make their decisions. She got up from the bed and stepped into the shower. The warm water helped in relieving her fears. She stepped out minutes later and opened her wardrobe. She selected an expensive crop top and a white safari, her blue stilettos laid on the marble floor. She checked her time; it was almost six in the morning. Her phone beeped, and she rushed to check who the caller was. It was a strange number; she swiped the green icon and waited for the caller to speak first.

"Miss Williams."

Her eyes popped out in excitement, "Mr. Chen, I had issues trying to reach you."

He chuckled with his rich baritone, "I was just thinking about you all night. Did you set up the team?"

She nodded, "Yeah, I was able to gather two of my best interns. They are marketing gurus and I strongly believe that we will figure stuff out today."

Marcus smiled, "That's the energy girl. How about I stop over today and run you through a new niche."

Sam hummed, "Which is?"

"Medicine, a cure for herpes and some other deadly STD. New inventions are in the market and we need to project the awareness to the community. It's a billion-dollar industry, so you are sure to get your ROI."

"I hear you Sir, but I just want to focus…"

"Diversify, remember. Right now, I could get you into the stock plan as a shareholder, but you need a plan that will enable you to flow through the waves seamlessly."

Sam breathed, "I am out of ideas."

"I will stop by at your company later in the day," Marcus promised.

Sam couldn't hide her excitement, "Thank you Mr. Chen."

"Yes, my little potato. And, enough with the Mr. Chen call me Marcus."

Hmm, that's a first!

"Okay Marcus, thanks so much for your help. I see you as my mentor."

"You are beautiful and strong," He complimented.

"Thank you."

The call ended, and she did a soft whistle and grabbed her car key. Marcus and she talked for about thirty minutes, and she needed to be in the office before eight. She stepped into her car and sped away. As she approached the building, the glowing sign *William Ventures* made her emotional and renewed her strength to give out the best and build an empire. As she stepped in, Becky was already passing with a tray of freshly brewed coffee.

"Morning Miss Williams," She greeted with a smile.

"A bright morning, Becky," She got a cup and took a sip. "Oh damn, this tastes good."

"It does tastes good," Becky replied.

"Morning, Miss Williams."

Sam turned to see Emily; she was in a dark corporate suit.

"You are looking dashing as usual," Emily complimented.

"Emily, I am happy to see you. We will have a meeting in an hour," Sam replied with a smile.

"Okay."

"My secretary will take you to the available rooms, choose any office that suits your comfort," Sam said.

"I like what you have done with this place," Emily looked around.

"Thousands of dollars went into the renovation," Sam replied.

Sam took the staircase and arrived at her office. She placed her bag by the side of the table and relaxed into the chair. She unlocked her system and scanned through the schedules. She had no meeting with any investors today, so she was free after the meeting with the team. She minimized the system and opened the word processing document to start preparing the agenda for the meeting. She heard a familiar knock, and she knew it was her secretary.

"A woman named Tara Simmons wants to see you."

A smile spread on Sam's face; her team was complete, and the operation won't be delayed.

The door opened, and Tara stepped in, "You have finally outdone yourself this time."

Sam smiled, "I am glad that you are here Tara."

"Where else would I be?"

"We have a thirteen sitter room. That will be the location for the board meeting," Sam said.

*

Thirty minutes later, she was done with the agenda for the meeting. She waited for a while before getting up. She picked up the files and her PC, stepped out of the office, and bounced like a Boss lady. She pushed the door open and everyone was already sitting. She moved over to the wall and pushed the board away, revealing a large screen. She plugged in the flash, and *Williams Venture* popped up. Everyone clapped, and for the first time, Sam felt a sense of pure pride.

"This is our company, our pride. Our success will motivate the world that nothing is impossible. I am glad we made it to this point. This company was birthed to transform this city and to transform ourselves. I put it to you, there would be no disappointment. No regrets, I would make sure of that."

The meeting continued, and the team shared ideas on the marketing strategy. The tech device was launched in the meeting, and the budget for advertisement was drawn and prepared. There was a live meeting with the tech owners as final paperwork was made to show that the prototype now belonged to *Williams Ventures.*

"We took a loan, a massive loan and it is going to be paid back. We will split the interest and the rest will go into developing the lands. Williams Ventures is rich in assets, I made sure of that. And once these landed properties are developed, these areas will attract investors who would come to do business. These investors will be ours and will agree to our terms," Sam said.

There was a brainstorming session which lasted for about an hour. And in the space of three hours, strategies were developed, decisions were made, and the operation was launched.

"Everyone will have to submit weekly reports on developments at their end. Let's get back to work," Samantha ordered.

**

Samantha was deep into a video meeting with a freelance surveyor for a project when the landline rang. She took an excuse and reached for it.

"Ma'am, a man named Marcus…"

"Let him in," Sam said. She wrapped up the meeting with the surveyor and switched off the system. She got up and straightened her clothes while staring at the door. She clicked a button on her table, and the door was unlocked. After some seconds, the door was unlocked, and Marcus stepped in with full glory. His brown hair was neatly curled, and he had a charming smile on his face. This time, he wasn't in a suit. He wore a t-shirt which clung to his body and a jean pant. There was a gold chain on his neck, and he kept smiling as he moved towards her. There was something different about him today, Sam noticed.

"Marcus," She called with a trembling voice.

"My little potato. You have done so well for yourself, I am proud of you," Marcus smiled.

"All thanks to your mentor ship. What can I offer you?" She asked.

He raised his hands up, "I am fine. Don't bother."

"Coffee will do," Sam reached for the landline and dialed the secretary's number, "Two cups of coffee, please?"

"So, what is your progress so far?" He leaned over on his chair.

"We are penetrating the market and we are going to take it by storm," She said.

Marcus nodded, "I believe that."

The secretary stepped in with two cups of coffee, the scent of the freshly brewed coffee made both of them smile.

"Damn," Marcus said in between his breath as he stared at Sam. Her face glowed, and she had this irresistible appeal. He stared into her hazel eyes; they were cutely shaped. He felt his heart tug in his chest as his gaze lingered on her pink caramel lips. He felt the urge to kiss those lips, but he had to fight it. Their eyes met, and he looked away. Sam noticed the tension and wondered why he was staring like that. She looked at his face; he was handsome with his brown skin. His eyes fluttered, giving him a dainty look. Their gaze met again, but they looked away as if their eyes emitted fire by contact.

Sam cleared her throat in a bid to lessen the tension, "You talked about moving into the medical niche?"

"Yes, yes," He replied in one breath and tilted forward, "The medical niche will favor your plan. Why? The detoxifier which you are trying to market will work in line with probably antibiotics and first generation pills. Research is coming in, the market is saturated already and sexual diseases are on the rise. The secret is, we search for deadly diseases, reach out to the CPR or World Health Organization (WHO) for a possible cure. We get a prototype, develop, get the drugs and pump it into the market."

Sam nodded, "That's right, but I will need help in outsourcing to WHO. I don't know how they operate."

Marcus nodded, "I will help you."

They smiled at each other, their gaze lingering.

CHAPTER 9

The newest CEO got up from the bed and stretched her body. She rushed into the bathroom and had a quick shower before dressing up. She had an appointment with Marcus in the morning, so she had to be early enough. Thirty minutes later, she arrived at the company to see Becky already sharing cups of steaming coffee. She got one and headed to her office.

Thirty minutes later, Marcus arrived. He was in a jersey neatly tucked into black pants. He wore his glasses, and that made him look nerdy.

"Welcome Marcus," She greeted.

He smiled at her, his gaze on her face. He noticed she doesn't have on any makeup, but she still looked very beautiful.

"Samantha, you look pretty this morning," His eyes settled on her chest. He noticed the shirt she wore revealed her cleavage. He swallowed hard and stared away.

Samantha noticed the tension; she saw the passion in his eyes and how his pupils dilated. She used her knuckles and rammed the table slowly to bring back his concentration. Marcus took a deep breath and scratched an itchy spot on his scalp.

"Were you able to prepare the outsourcing document?" She asked.

"Yeah, we are going to submit a soft copy of this to the official email of WHO. But, we are going to be willing to work with any prototype they give us. And, since WHO might not be interested in the major proceeds of the drugs, we need to prove to them that we are capable of handling the major distribution," Marcus explained.

Sam got the file and read through it; she had some issues understanding some stuff. Marcus put her through while she updated her proposal.

"How is the tech device sales faring?" Marcus asked.

Sam smiled, "So far, we are penetrating the market. We have made up to six hundred sales and I am about to place order for new products. Thanks for everything Marcus."

Marcus grumbled and leaned back on the chair, his gaze still on Sam's face.

Sam raised an eyebrow, "Is there a problem?"

He shrugged, "No, I'm just admiring."

Sam nodded and buried her head into the file, she knew Marcus was checking her out, and she loved it. She raised her eyes occasionally to look at his face; he practically glowed.

"I was thinking, since cancer is the most prevalent condition, we can make research on it and submit some findings to WHO. We could spare a space for a medical professional, get some rare drugs into the market," Sam said.

Marcus nodded, "That's a pretty good idea."

Sam clasped her hands together in excitement, "I am finally loving this niche. Maybe I should put a hold on the estate development."

"No, carry everything along with the right strategy," Marcus said.

"See," Sam got up from her seat with the tablet, "There is something I discovered."

She stood close to Marcus and bent low, "Part of New Orleans is really in need of tech. Probably the next order could be shipped there."

Marcus nodded, "Congrats baby girl. The sales looks good, your people are showing great team work."

Sam was too close for comfort as her chest brushed against Marcus' elbow. He felt the warmth across his chest and stiffened. Sam enjoyed the sensation, but she had to leave her seat. As she starts to walk away, Marcus held her elbow.

"What do I get for being a mentor?" He asked.

Sam thought for a while, "You will be duly compensated."

He chuckled, "Three million dollars or a kiss."

"Huh?" Samantha gasped.

He shrugged and got up, "You heard me right."

He walked over to her and slowly placed his hands on her waist, "From the very first day you stepped into the ted fun event, I knew I had found love. You are an embodiment of strength, grace, and power. You have the king's blood flowing in your veins."

She was stunned and kept staring at him, "Marcus…"

"Shhh," He placed a finger on her lips. He closed in and caught her lips with his. Sam melted completely under his firm grip. Her breathing increased as she tried to match his pace. The dude was a fast kisser, but she enjoyed it. She had always had this fantasy in her head that Asian guys were good kissers. After about a minute, he broke the kiss.

"I am sorry," He swallowed.

She was shy, but her confidence took charge, "No need to be apologizing. We both wanted it."

"Looks like I forced myself on you," Marcus sat back.

Sam moved over to her table and rested her palms on it; she wasn't ready for this route her life was navigating.

"Let's finalize the proposal so that I can hand the file over to you," Marcus said.

Sam raised her gaze, "I thought you wanted to handle the submissions and everything?"

Marcus chuckled, "Look. I don't want to be a distraction. I don't want it to seem like I am taking advantage of you, okay?"

Sam lowered her ass on the chair, "Damn! I don't know what to say."

Marcus pulled out the files and scribbled a few contents on them, "You will have to get a medical professional to go through the contents. Before we submit it to WHO and then, the prototype, sales... we go from there."

Sam nodded, "Thank you, Marcus. I may not share the same feelings as you but I admire you greatly and I still want your mentor ship. Don't just go, please."

Marcus smiled, "I never said I was going, just wanted out from the distraction."

"We are adults and we can work without letting this," She gestured, "Distract us."

"Okay," He replied.

"I actually thought you were married," She said and tilted forward.

"Presumably, people think I am in my forties. I'm not married, I had a failed relationship. That was seven years ago. You Europe girls seem to be a whole bunch of trouble."

She smiled, "Ladies all over the world are bunch of troubles."

"Not in China," He said.

She giggled, "Don't you dare make exceptions."

**

Sam pressed the last key on the system and clicked sent. She logged out from the WHO official website and cracked her knuckles. A smile appeared on her face as she remembered the kiss she shared with Marcus. She stared at the empty chair before her; he had left two hours ago for an urgent meeting. She shook her thoughts to one side as she thought of what to have for lunch. Some ice cream will be nice; she got up and made for the door, but her secretary stepped in.

"Ma'am, there is an investor waiting to see you."

Sam's heart skipped, "An investor?"

"Yeah, he came alone. Frank Mitchell," The secretary replied.

"Interesting. Bring him in," Sam ordered and moved to her seat.

Two seconds later, a tall and well-built man walked into the office. He had a cocky smile dancing around his lips as he adjusted the buttons of his jacket.

"Miss Williams," He gave a mock bow and let himself on the chair.

"Frank Mitchell, good to have you," She replied.

He crossed his leg and ran his fingers through his short-cropped salt and pepper hair. He grinned and leaned back on the chair.

"My team was here at the beginning of the week," He said.

Sam thought for some seconds, "Mines and Crafts companies?"

"Exactly, I work there as the sales executive," He sat erect.

"You are welcome. We have launched our tech device in the market and we get positive feedback. We are looking into creating a cure for cancer and…"

"You need investors?" He asked.

Sam nodded, "Yes, we do."

"This tech device is produced and distributed by your company right?" He asked.

Sam nodded, wondering why he was asking questions.

"Did you get to run test with the prototype?" He asked.

Sam nodded, "Our tech partners did a thorough laboratory check on the device and sent reports. I monitored the reports myself."

Frank uncrossed his leg, "You have no background in tech. What makes you think you were not fooled?"

"Excuse me?" She tilted forward.

"I mean no offence; I mean I am willing to key into your vision. But, I feel you are too fast paced."

"Mr. Mitchell, I really do not understand you," Sam was getting pissed.

"What does this device do in particular?" He rubbed his hands together.

"It helps to clear the system of toxic waste. It is an essential medical tool and if you use it, you will love it," Sam said, hoping this dude would leave.

"If I use it, I will love it?" He asked.

Sam nodded, "Certainly."

"Have you used it yourself?" He asked.

Sam took a deep breath, "What do you want?"

"A young pretty lady starts up a firm and goes into one of the most technical niche of business..."

"What do you suppose I do?" She snapped.

"Easy, my company is looking at investing a huge amount of money here. I don't want them making a mistake."

"They won't be making a mistake," She replied. She took a deep breath, "I am sorry for snapping at you."

"There is no problem. My company will get back to you soon," He smiled and got up.

CHAPTER 10

A black sedan pulled up in front of a huge building. Frank Mitchell killed the engine and stepped out of the car. It had rained last night, and there was dew everywhere. He closed the car, straightened his jacket, and walked into the firm. He stepped into the elevator and waited patiently as it slid up and landed at the apex corridor. He stepped out of the elevator and rapped a knock on the door. It was unlocked, and he moved inside.

"Mr. Mitchell," The CEO adjusted his spectacles.

Frank unbuttoned his jacket and sat down, "I met the young CEO yesterday." Frank pulled out a picture folder and placed it on the table.

The CEO of Mines and Crafts, a man in his late fifties, picked up the folder and opened it. He stared at the pictures for a while before dropping it.

"The first picture is a woman with a swollen stomach. The doctors reported an abnormal abdominal growth of a tissue in her stomach. That happened after she used a tech device produced by Williams Ventures. The same thing happened again with the aged man and the pretty teenage girl."

The CEO leaned back on the chair, "Are you sure about this?"

Frank nodded, "I spoke with the patients at the hospital before they died."

"And they claimed the detoxifying device caused it?" The CEO asked.

"What else would it be?" Frank asked.

"Was there any test result to show that something in the device is harmful?" The CEO asked.

"Sir, please. Now is not the time for questions. I need to write articles warning the public about the device," Frank said.

"It's not in your place to do that now. We haven't gotten a confirmation that the tech device caused it actually. I have used it and I haven't noticed any irregularities in my system," The CEO said.

Frank nodded, "Sir, your system isn't the same as the others."

"But, I believe we started using it at the same duration. Many people have used it, we are supposed to hear of massive dead records," The CEO said.

"A young lady is…."

"You sound quite jealous, Frank," The CEO pulled out his spectacles, "You are acting like Miss Samantha Williams offended you."

"I don't want her over zealousness to get ahead of her. She is trying by all means to be successful."

"Frank, you need to get your fact straight. This girl has done you no wrong."

"She has done the society wrong," Frank got up and picked up the folders. He headed to his office and pulled out his system. He opened an anonymous media account and typed:

This is to inform the general public that the tech device called 'Detoxifier' produced by Williams Ventures is fake and dangerous to the system. Eight people have lost their lives already, and we are calling on the government to cease her license and stop her from operating.

Written by:

Anonymous

**

It was midday, and Sam stepped out for lunch with Becky. They were in a cafe sipping wine and eating some puddings.

"So, you kissed Marcus?" Becky asked.

"Yeah, he made a move first. And, I couldn't resist," Sam replied.

"The dude loves you," Becky said.

Sam shrugged, "I don't share the same feelings. I admire him greatly, he is intelligent and rich."

Sam's phone beeped; it was Tara on the line. She swiped the green icon and placed it on her ear.

"Miss Williams, check your Instagram. There is a news making round and it is tarnishing."

"Tara, calm down and take a breather. What is happening?"

"There is an article with pictures and claims that our tech device is killing people. It has your picture tagged murderer," Tara said.

A sharp headache passed through Sam's head, ''Let me check."

Becky noticed the change in Sam's countenance, "Any problems."

Sam logged into her Instagram, and the notifications were mind-blowing. She had seven hundred tags and six thousand messages. She went through her news feed, and her knees buckled in fear.

"Samantha, what is it?"

"Someone is trying to tarnish my image" Sam's face went pale and she almost threw up. "Finish the food, I will be back."

Sam's heart was beating as she rushed through the express and headed to the office. She saw Tara and Emily roaming the hallway.

"This isn't looking right," Emily said.

Sam held her forehead; it seemed her head was about to burst. "Go back to your work; I will get to the root of this."

Sam held the rails of the stairs and tried to climb up, but her knees wobbled. She steadied her gaze and climbed through. She entered her office and sat down. She noticed that the office landline had been ringing nonstop by concerned people. She opened her Instagram account and debunked the rumors. There was no way the tech device was responsible for their deaths. Over one thousand people have used it so far, and there were no deaths. She tried tracing the source of the message, but it was written by an anonymous sender. She called her partnering tech company to hear from them, and they convinced her that the prototype was perfect. She got up and paced around the office.

She dialed Marcus' number and waited for it to ring. The phone rang, and it was answered later.

"Someone is spreading false information about the tech device. He claimed it killed three people," Sam said.

"If it killed three people, it isn't the tech device," Marcus said.

Sam rested her head on the chair, "I am fed up with all this. Do you think it's from a competitor?"

"Yes. I think so," Marcus replied.

"I have debunked the claims. I won't pay attention to it," She said.

"It might affect your sales; hope you know that. I am not saying this to make you feel bad, I just want you to brace yourself for what is coming. There will be a lot of challenges."

"I am ready. I need a favor from you."

"Okay?"

"I need a good techie; I need to trace the source of the message."

"I will send a contact," He replied.

**

Samantha sat on a swivel chair, staring at the system in front of her. Occasionally, she stared at her phone as she was waiting for the report from the tech man she hired. She just noticed that the sales had reduced and the bar charts went down. She rubbed her palms as she was getting nervous. Her phone beeped, and her heart skipped in anticipation. She picked it up and swiped the green icon.

"Any new development?" She asked.

A slight cough was heard in the background, "The message has gone viral and I am still working on the source. But, I have been able to trace the hospital where the alleged victims were. Would you love to pay them a visit?"

"Certainly," Sam got up and picked up her car key, "Keep working."

She picked up her other phone and dialed Becky's number, "Meet me outside."

Ten minutes later, she was in the car with Becky. Sam kept driving in silence and was grumbling words to herself.

Becky coughed, "I saw the message. Who would do something like that?"

Sam shook her head, "No idea."

Becky folded her arms, "Do you think Mr. Johnson is behind this?"

Sam shook her head, "That's not his way of doing things."

Becky nodded, "We will get to the root of this."

Fifteen minutes later, Sam pulled up in front of the hospital. It was a bungalow situated around a small grass area. Sam observed the hospital for a while; she could see nurses stepping in and out. Sam pushed the door open, and they stepped out of the car. They walked briskly to the entrance and moved to the counter.

"I need to see the medical director," Sam said, seizing the nurses with her eyes.

"Do you have an appointment with him?" The head nurse asked.

"Yeah, I am Miss Samantha Williams, the CEO of Williams Ventures. There are claims that my tech device killed three people. Those people were admitted in this hospital."

"I cannot grant you access now, except you have an appointment with him," The nurse said.

"Keep your mouth shut, please. This is a delicate matter and your hospital released the report. Link us to him now," Becky glared at them.

It seemed her voice did the magic, and the head nurse scampered to get the landline, "Ohhh, let me call him."

Sam breathed and turned her gaze to the woman who was wheeled into a ward.

"He is in his office. That way," The nurse pointed.

Sam and Becky walked to the office, and Sam pushed the door in without knocking. This scared the sixty-two-year-old man, and he pulled out his glasses and glared at the two ladies.

"Who the hell are you both?"

"Doctor, I am Samantha Williams. The CEO of Williams Ventures".

"Ohhh, how can I help you?" The doctor asked.

Sam walked over to his table, pulled out her phone, and placed it in front of his face.

"Start explaining," She said.

The man took a deep breath, "These people, I remember them. They died of hernia."

"Hernia? I thought you said the tech device killed them?" Sam glared.

"Two of the victims used the device. But, they didn't die from it. I didn't give any report about it. I was shocked to see it online," the doctor replied.

"Then a member of your staff did?" Becky asked.

"Who else, apart from your staff knew about the incident?" Sam asked.

"A certain man, he brought one of them. She claimed she suffered a shock after using the tech device," the doctor said. "After running checks, she suffered from goiter and the device triggered a shock. But, she didn't actually die by the device."

Sam took a deep breath, "I need to find who wrote the post," Sam slid her business card on the table. "Call me when you get a development."

CHAPTER 11

Sam killed the engine in front of her apartment. She rested her head on the chair and caressed her forehead. She had a throbbing headache already as a result of the stress. After she left the doctor's office, she visited her legal consultant for a brief meeting. She also had a press conference to debunk the rumors and also assured the general public that the device was safe to be used. She unlocked the car and stepped out. The sole of her feet was beginning to hurt, and she walked slowly to the house. She unlocked the door, and her dog wagged its tail and approached her. She bent down, played with his head before relaxing on the chair. She reached for her phone and sent a message to her employees. She was going to address them tomorrow.

She dialed Marcus' number and waited for it to ring. It rang for seven consecutive times and wasn't answered. She stood up and walked slowly to her room. She unlocked the tap and waited for the water to trickle down her body. As she was bathing, she heard a knock on the door. She listened carefully, the knock persisted, and she got out of the bathtub and wrapped a towel around her body. She went to the door and unlocked it.

"Jesus Christ," She gasped. Her mouth hung open as she saw Marcus standing before her with a bottle of wine.

"Are you going to let me inside?" He asked, his mouth hung open as he stared at the outline of her chest. Her glowing skin was wrapped in a towel. He blinked and stared back at her face.

Samantha was conscious of his gaze on her body, she stepped back a bit. "Come in."

Marcus chuckled and walked into the sitting room. His eyes roamed everywhere, and he lowered himself into the sofa.

"Let me go and change," She said and rushed back into the room. She wore a polo over loose pants and stepped out. She moved into the kitchen and returned with two wine glasses.

"You got a dog. Cute little thing," Marcus said.

"Yeah, he is my companion in this cold lonely flat," Sam replied and placed the glasses on the table. "What are we celebrating?"

Marcus uncorked the bottle with a bright smile, "We are celebrating you."

Sam scoffed, "Me?"

"Yeah, you. The way you handled everything today. I saw the press conference; you are a definition of strength."

Sam smiled and shrugged, "I just did what I had to do."

Marcus poured the contents into the glasses and lifted his, "To strength."

"To strength," Sam replied.

Marcus sat back on the chair, "When I started my firm, the first few months, I ran into issues with my investors. The issues were scandalous and it involved the corps. I was depressed and I stayed indoors for weeks even though I wasn't guilty."

"People respond to issues differently."

Marcus nodded, "You are strong and that I appreciate."

"Thank you. I need to be strong for my team and for myself."

They drank in silence, and Sam kept avoiding his gaze.

"When you called me, what did you wanted to say," he asked.

Sam shrugged, "I don't know, I guess I just needed someone to talk to."

Marcus nodded, "I am glad that you found me worthy."

Sam smiled, "You are a blessing to my life. I will always be grateful to have met you."

Marcus laughed, "Enough with the gratitude. We are in each other's life, that's what matters."

They kept drinking, and Marcus fixed his gaze on her face, "You are glowing, despite the stress."

"You think?" Sam raised her gaze.

"I know," Marcus replied.

After minutes of drinking, Marcus got up. He moved slowly towards Sam, making her heart beat in confusion and excitement. She steadied her gaze on the ground as she couldn't stare at his fiery gaze. He bent low and picked up a flash.

"Here."

Disappointment drawn on Sam's face, she thought that he wanted to kiss her. She breathed a sigh and took the flash from him. Marcus inserted his hands into his pocket with a blank look on his face.

"I will be leaving," he shrugged.

She nodded, "Yes, it is late. You have a good night."

"Thanks for having me," he said.

She nodded, "Thanks for the wine. It is one of the best I have ever tasted."

"That's pure vintage. It is a quality product."

She squeezed her shoulders and stared at her fingers like a high school kid. "Let me see you off."

"Okay," Marcus shrugged.

They both stepped out together, and they moved towards Marcus' car.

Sam turned and stared at him, "How did you know my house address?"

"When you called, I tracked it," He replied.

"What?" She raised her gaze.

"Just kidding. I have something to admit. My personal bodyguard noticed how attached we were, he decided to keep tabs on you for security reasons. Not like I doubted you, but he had to. He told me after that you were no threat."

Sam nodded, "Do I look like one?"

"Heard of sleeper agents?" He asked.

"No," She replied.

"In time past, some politicians would pay pretty ladies to seduce their opponents and sleep with them."

Sam nodded, "I see where this is coming from. But, you actually seduced me, didn't you?"

"I didn't," They both broke into a feat of laughter.

"Good night Marcus," she said.

"Good night Samantha," he said and hopped into his car.

He ignited the engine and raced out of the premises. Sam watched until he disappeared out of sight. She took a deep breath and stepped back into the house. As she stepped into her room, she heard her phone ringing.

"Hello Becky."

"I know you don't sleep early. Why didn't you pick up your phone?"

Sam rolled her eyes and sat on the foot of the bed, "I was with Marcus."

"Damn, he came to your place? You are in for a long thing. How are you faring?"

"Becky, not tonight. Go away, I need to sleep," Sam replied dreamily.

"Easy on yourself, girlfriend," Becky said soothingly.

"Mug," Sam said aloud as she searched for her toothbrush. She brushed her mouth and stepped into the bath. Minutes later, she was standing close to her car. Before she ignited the engine, she logged into her Instagram account and viewed her press conference again. It was making the desired impact. An idea occurred to her; she smiled, stepped on the gas pedal and drove speedily. She arrived at her firm some minutes before eight. She greeted a few of her staff and moved into her office. She picked up her journal and scripted a few agenda for the meeting. An hour later, she stepped into the conference room with vigor and confidence. She stared at her team members' faces before clearing her throat.

"What defines the strength of a man is his ability to survive hard times. Yesterday, I was able to trace the hospital and I discovered that those people died as a result of other complications. That is to say, anyone who wrote the anonymous article is an enemy of the company. But, that shouldn't stop us from working very hard," Sam said.

The meeting ended after an hour, and Sam returned to her office. She kept on monitoring the proceeds of the tech device and the rate it was procured. So far, she hasn't received any update about any death. Her phone beeped, and she picked it up; it was the techie on the line.

"Any update?" She asked.

"I have been able to trace the account and it has been deleted already. The IP address isn't active. That means anyone who wrote that didn't want to be traced."

Sam nodded, "Okay, thank you very much."

The call went dead; she leaned back on the chair and stared at the prototype being displayed on the screen. Her phone beeped again, and she stared at the screen. It was the tech guy.

"I guess you will want to get a word or two from the family of the deceased."

Sam shifted forward, "Yes I would."

"I will drop some names to you. You can take it from there."

Some minutes later, some names and addresses were dropped into her contacts. She dialed a security agency and paid for an escort. If the family thinks her product is responsible for the death of their loved ones, they might not want to listen to an explanation before they start venting their anger.

"Becky, we have some places to be," Sam said.

An hour later, they were on their way to Austin. They arrived after an hour, and Sam directed the driver to the first residence. Sam stepped out and was being flagged by two armed men.

Sam entered the house and met an aged man, they had a conversation, and Sam was able to convince the man that her device wasn't responsible for his granddaughter's death. There was a live interview, and Sam proceeded to the next residence. After five hours, she was able to speak with the families affected. She gifted each of them the device and also promised to check on them.

CHAPTER 12

Frank Mitchell groaned as he browsed through his iPad. He was surprised at the way Samantha handled the whole issue. He got up from his bed and moved into the sitting room. He opened his drawer and pulled out a sim card, which he inserted into his phone and logged on to activate the Instagram account. He opened his keyboard and typed:

Do not fall for Samantha Williams' tricks; she is killing the masses slowly with her tech devices. Her license must be ceased, and her firm must be closed down. People are dying, and she has restricted their family from talking. Details, proofs, and pictures will be coming later.

He typed it and sent it. He pulled off the sim card and returned it into the drawer. He got up to see a missed call notification on his second phone. It was the doctor calling.

"Hey doctor," he called in high spirits.

"Samantha Williams was here the previous day," he said.

Frank took a deep breath, "What did you tell her?"

"The truth," the doctor shrugged, "Frank, why are you trying to discredit her?"

"I believe I owe you no explanation. A young lady shouldn't be allowed to distribute sensitive items," Frank said and got up.

"But the devices are safe, I recommended it for my patients," the doctor said.

An idea occurred to Frank, "I need you to do something for me. I will pay you thirty grand."

"What is it?" the doctor asked.

"I'll meet you in the hospital soon," Frank got up and walked into his room. He had a quick change, wore his jacket, and stepped out of the house. He got into his car and raced to the hospital. He arrived some minutes later and breezed into the doctor's office.

"I hope you never told Miss Williams about my involvement?" Frank asked as he stepped into the office.

The doctor shook his head in a negative, "I never did."

"Good. I need to see the patient that used the device," Frank said.

The doctor led him into one of the wards; Frank stared around. Few of the people in it were on life-supporting machines. He went to a lady who lay limply on the bed.

"Hey," Frank greeted.

The lady turned slowly to him, "Hey."

"I want you to do a little task for me and I will take care of your medical expenses," Frank offered.

"What is it?" She asked.

Frank signaled the doctor to help the girl to rise. Frank got closer to her and folded his arms.

"I need you to say something while I make a video. I want you to tell the world that the tech device released by Williams Ventures is toxic and it is killing you slowly. Can you do that?" Frank asked.

"What's in for me?" She shrugged.

"Twenty grand and I will take care of your bills," Frank offered.

In an hour, he made ten videos of different sick people. He gave all of them money and thanked the doctor. He headed back into his car and drove home. He moved into his sitting room, retrieved the sim, and inserted it into his device. He activated the account and uploaded the videos. As soon as the upload was complete, he smiled and deactivated the account.

"Okay Sam, let's see how you figure this out," He said with a mischievous grin.

*

Sam was doing some laundry when she heard her phone beep. The beeping continued, and she rushed to the kitchen table where she placed it. It was a call from Becky. She swiped the green icon and placed it on her ear.

"There are videos trending about the device. Our enemies are at it again."

Sam ended the call and switched on her data, the first message that popped up from her news app was:

Samantha Williams, a potential terrorist.

Samantha Williams is looking to destroy the state with her biological weapon.

Samantha Williams should be probed by the US government.

Sam chuckled and placed the phone back on the table; her hands began to shiver. Her phone beeped again, and she picked it up; messages that contained threats of court proceedings and warnings popped up on her phone. Her phone was blowing up.

"Please God," she gasped and leaned on the wall.

Her heart was beginning to slam against her chest, and her feet could barely hold her weight. Her phone beeped again, it was Emily on the line. She picked it up and slid the green icon.

"Boss, we are in trouble."

Sam nodded with a bitter smile, "I know we are."

"No, much bigger trouble," Emily said.

Sam chuckled, "Could my weekend get any better?"

"The US government has placed the company's license on a temporary hold."

"That's bullshit. Why would they? For an accusation that holds no weight?" Sam asked.

"We need to do something quick," Emily said.

"I'll be heading to Washington tomorrow. I need to sort this out quickly."

As the call went off, another came on. It was the tech guy; she swiped the green icon and placed it on her ear.

"I may have traced the account making these posts."

"Who is behind it?" Sam asked.

"I don't know yet. But, that will be known before the end of next week. Right now, I am working on debunking those videos and making sure it is shadow banned. There will be restrictions on accounts that will share the videos."

Sam nodded, "Thank you very much. I need one more favor."

"Okay?"

"I need a 2 o'clock flight to Washington DC."

"That will be done."

Sam took a deep breath; the calls coming in were blowing up her phone. She went back to her room and reached for her laptop. She logged in and initiated a conference call with her team. One by one, their face popped up on the screen.

"A lot is going on right now and I am trying my best not to lose my sanity. But, we will be fine."

"Yes, we will," they replied.

"I will be travelling to Washington today. I need to clear this mess."

**

At dusk, Samantha Williams arrived at the airport in Washington. Her tech guy had already booked a hotel and sent her the booking address. She needed to be in the white house at dawn the next day. Maybe she could have a private chat with the secretary of the parliament. She picked up a taxi and arrived at her hotel some minutes later. She paid some dollars to the receptionist and headed to her room. As she stepped in, she was greeted by a soothing smell of lavender. The warm serenity of the room brought a bit of solace, and she fell on the bed.

She reached for her phone and dialed Marcus' number. It rang but wasn't answered. She felt he might just show up at her door with a bottle of wine and soothing words. Her eyelids felt heavy as she never had a proper sleep in the past few days. She closed her eyes and allowed herself to be carried away.

Some hours later, she woke up before dawn and had a brief shower. She waited for the day to brighten, and then she ordered breakfast. After eating, she stepped out of her hotel room, booked a taxi, and headed to the White House. As the car breezed through the cold street of Washington, she could see people dressed in church wears and heading to their various parishes. She cracked her knuckles in anticipation; she would see the secretary to the parliament who thrash things out about her company. She had to draw strength from the inside for her team and the company. Williams Ventures won't fall, not under her watch.

CHAPTER 13

Kings Consolidated

Mr. Johnson stared at the figures on his laptop screen; his recent investment wasn't doing well. He clicked on the exit key and leaned back on the chair. This is one of the reasons he missed Samantha Williams; the lady knew her job. He had never lost any major investment. He closed his eyes and tried to envision her pretty face; he had missed her. Her soft, tender voice, her smiles, her scents. He never knew that she had the balls to start up her own company. He opened his eyes to prevent himself from daydreaming. Samantha's tech device has taken over the market, and his own device was struggling to stay relevant. The lady just knew the right thing to do at the right time. A knock on his office door distracted him, and he raised his gaze to the door.

It was his executive assistant who just stepped in. "Mrs. Angela Davis," he says.

"Mr. Johnson, the files for the presentation are ready," she said.

"Good. I will be at the board room soon."

The sound from the television distracted them; they raised their gaze to the screen as particular news caught their attention.

Williams Ventures stands a risk of losing their license as rumors that the tech device is killing people. Many people are now looking at the device as a biological weapon.

"Bullshit! This is a work of some charlatan trying to discredit her," Mr. Johnson said and picked up the remote; he turned off the screen.

Angela shrugged, "But, there have been videos about people getting sick because of the device. Though my husband used it about a month ago and we are yet to see any downside."

"I know Samantha; she has a good heart. She won't hurt anyone or produce a biological weapon like they put it," Mr. Johnson said.

Angela shrugged, "Poor girl, I just hope she will be able to find her way out of this."

Mr. Johnson nodded, "I trust her, and she would be able to handle things perfectly. I mean, look at her company in barely three months. She has achieved what took me a year to do."

"You have trust despite the way she left? And, she also took some of your best staff from you," Angela said as she arranged the files.

Mr. Johnson took a deep breath, "I was too hard on the poor girl. I just let my frustrations and hard demeanor get in the way. I pushed her to the wall and I regret every single bit of it."

Angela brushed over her curly red hair, "Don't you think you are always too hard on your staff? I mean most times; you act like the Devil's advocate."

Mr. Johnson eyed her and took a deep breath. Angela was the only person that could scold him. She was one of the founding staff of the company and was a mother figure to him.

"Samantha said a lot of hurtful words before she left. I feel she had been meaning to say that," Angela dragged a chair and lowered herself into it. She fixed her stern look on him.

"Yeah, I deserve everything she said. She has been my best staff and I am proud of the woman she is becoming. I have a confession to make."

Angela raised her brow, "I am listening."

"I was kind of obsessed with Sam and it just triggered my anger for her. When she left, I have been keeping tabs of her daily moves. I have been looking for a way to apologize to her but my gut keeps failing me," he said.

Angela nodded, "It's not too late, okay?"

"You think? There is no need for apologies again, she is doing well for herself," Mr. Johnson said.

Angela shrugged, "If you say so. I just hope she won't lose her license because of this conspiracy theories flying around."

Mr. Johnson nodded, "She won't. I am sure of that."

**

The airplane landed at Dallas Airport, and Sam stepped out of it. She sighed in relief as she was back. She couldn't go to the office as she knew that they must have closed operations by now. It was almost five in the evening. She flagged a taxi and entered into it. As the taxi sped through the road, she recounted her experience in Washington. She was able to speak with the secretary that Sunday, and they went through a lot of evidence. That meeting alone saved her license from being temporarily withheld. She was sure to get to the person making those claims and posting those videos. She dialed Becky's number and informed her that she was back. Some minutes later, she arrived home and settled into a chair. She had checked her dog in with a vet and would be picking him up later in the day. She moved into the bathroom and had her bath before stepping into the sitting room to see a movie. She tried dialing Marcus' number, but he couldn't be reached.

A knock distracted her; could it be Marcus? Maybe, Becky. She got up and moved over to the door, she unlocked it, and her mouth hung open in surprise.

"Angela?"

The short woman's stern expression widened into a bright smile, "My girl."

"I…am…" Sam couldn't complete her statement; she jumped into Angela's arms and remained there.

"Oh, my girl. You just left."

Sam shook her head, "I am sorry. Let us go in."

They stepped into the sitting room. "I know you don't like fruit juice and I have no wine here. Maybe I should just make an order."

"No, I am fine. Sit," Angela ordered.

Sam sat close to her, "How is the company faring?"

Angela nodded, "It is cool. You never even told me you started yours. You made me an enemy over night."

"I am sorry. It was just too much. I was ashamed to face you because of how I left."

"No, my baby girl. You are wrong. Johnson was a thorn in your flesh that I know."

Sam nodded, "How is he?"

"He is missing you greatly."

**

"That's a lie," Sam chuckled.

"Trust me; he hasn't stopped talking about how he misses you. Turns out he's been keeping tabs on you."

Sam laughed, "I have never seen anyone as confused as he is. Why has he been keeping tabs on me? Dude made my life a living hell in his company."

"Maybe he likes you. Rather liked you and didn't know how to say it."

"So, he had to use the language of hatred to communicate love?" Sam asked.

"Mr. Johnson can be a difficult man," Angela said.

"He can be? He is," Sam said.

"News about you came up on the TV. I saw the genuine care and love in his eyes. He is rooting for your success."

Sam shrugged, "That's very kind of him. Tell him thank you."

"He wants to apologize," Angela said.

Sam moaned, "He shouldn't add to my problems, he shouldn't."

"Calm down baby. How are you holding up with everything that is happening?" Angela asked.

Sam leaned back and took a deep breath, "I just came back from Washington not too long ago. I spoke with the Secretary of the Parliament. We were able to resolve the issues and…"

"I think someone is trying to frame you. Or perhaps bring you down, maybe a rival?"

"I almost thought it was Mr. Johnson."

"No girl. He won't do that."

Sam nodded, "I can't wait to get my hands on who ever the person is. He has caused me a lot already."

"The person has given you quite a bit of publicity. Like we use to say, no publicity is bad publicity. You just need to know how to handle the heat."

Sam nodded, "I missed you."

"I have missed you too my baby girl. I know you have been going through a lot, momma is here for you."

CHAPTER 14

An eighteen-year-old Thomas stared at his wristwatch; the sole of his feet was sore as he had been walking for over three hours. He had no money in his pocket to pick a taxi, and he was starving greatly. He stood under a tree and waited to regain his strength. There was a water fountain in the middle of the road, and he walked over to it and climbed the steps. As he almost made it to the water, a cop on the side of the street cocked his gun at him and ordered him to step down from the water fountain. Thomas groaned and contemplated; the officer was far and would take up to five minutes before reaching him. He decided to drink the water before rushing down. He climbed onto the next step, used his palms to fetch the water. He took it to his mouth and drank a little of it; he noticed the water was salty. He drank some more and saw the cop running towards him. He used his water bottle, fetched as much as he could before he stepped down. By this time, the cop was closing down on him. He ran into the next street and hid in between the cabs. After a while, he pulled out his hood and wore it over his head.

Two hours later, he arrived home. He lived in one of the cottages in New Orleans. He pushed the door open and stepped in. There was an old creaky mattress lying on the floor. He pulled off his clothes and lowered himself slowly. He had gone for a job interview, and he ended up not getting the job. He tried to beg for some cash, but he was thrown out of the facility. Now, he was weak and starving.

Thomas Johnson was born an orphan and was adopted into the orphanage at the age of six. He endured a whole lot of suffering and pain. For every single meal he ate, he had to fight for it. For every comfort he enjoyed, he had to fight for it. The scar on his head was as a result of a fight he had with an older guy in the orphanage.

"This is my space, I got here first and I haven't been served yet," Thomas tried to struggle with another boy in the refectory. The other boy was four years older than him and very energetic.

"Thomas, I will smite your head against the pillar. As a matter of fact, there will be no food for you this week".

Thomas tried to struggle, and the boy grabbed him and slammed his head against the pillar, causing Thomas to bleed. That week, Thomas didn't have a meal, and he had to learn how to fight. He grew up with the belief that the world wasn't capable of loving anyone.

He blinked back to reality as his stomach rumbled violently. He had to get up and look for food, or he would starve.

The Present

Kings Consolidated

Mr. Johnson blinked back to reality as a knock sounded on his door. He took a deep breath and straightened the cuffs of his shirt. Angela stepped into the office. She looked at him.

"Still brooding?" She asked.

Mr. Johnson shrugged, "I am fine."

"I have been able to prepare the documents for the project," she handed the folder to Mr. Johnson.

Mr. Johnson browsed through the folder, "I have never ventured into something of this nature before. And, I don't even know how to interpret this prototype."

Angela nodded, "But, we can't let this contract off our hands."

"So, what's your opinion?" Mr. Johnson stared at her.

"I feel we should bring Samantha on it. She will know how to handle this best."

Mr. Johnson chuckled, "Samantha doesn't work here any longer, and how do you suppose I bring her in."

"It doesn't matter; you both can work on it together. The most important thing is nailing this project and putting smiles on our investor's face."

Mr. Johnson took a deep breath, "I don't think this will work. I will see how to partner with another company."

"And, risk a failure? Samantha Williams is our surest bet," Angela said and walked out of the office.

Thomas Johnson folded his fist and groaned; he picked up his phone and searched his work contact. He hoped he wouldn't find her number so that he could consider other options. And, there it was, staring at him in the face. He dialed the number in bated breath and waited for it to ring.

It was answered, and Mr. Johnson's heart started beating. There was silence for a moment until he cleared his throat and spoke out.

"Miss Samantha Williams."

"Mr. Thomas Johnson, how convenient for you to reach out to me."

"I am calling for business. I need your help on a medical project."

Sam chuckled, "What's in it for me?"

"If it is successful, you are getting a million dollar from it," he said.

"That's nice. But, you have to work on my terms."

Mr. Johnson tilted forward, "What does that mean?"

"I said it has to be on my terms. I make the decisions and I call the shots."

Mr. Johnson smirked, "And, why should I agree to that?"

"Then, I'll pass. I have too much on my table to deal with, I can't add yours to it," Sam said.

"Easy please, okay. I agree. When will we be having our first meeting?"

Sam thought for a while, "This weekend, at the Chinese restaurant. I will send you the address".

"Okay, Boss," Mr. Johnson replied.

Sam smiled, hearing that reply was weird.

"Do we have a deal?" Sam asked.

"Yes, we do," he replied.

The call was ended, and he took a deep breath of relief. Right now, he was looking forward to seeing Samantha. He had missed her, missed everything about her. His mood was now lightened, and he reached for his laptop to continue working.

CHAPTER 15

Samantha stepped out of her office with mixed feelings. She kept wondering why Thomas Johnson, the High Lord of all, would need her help in a project. She even wondered why he would agree to her terms. She greeted a few other staff and raced down the stairs. Today was quite exhausting, and she was glad it was the weekend. She somehow felt excited that she would be seeing Thomas Johnson again; she couldn't wait to see the defeated look on his face. Twenty minutes later, she arrived home and had a brief shower. She retired to the bed and dozed off.

She woke up at dawn and stared at the wall clock. She had a meeting with Thomas in an hour, and she needed to be quick. One thing she knew about him; he was a punctual person. She got into the kitchen and made some fries, made coffee, and sat down to eat. She never enjoyed the fries because cooking wasn't one of her strong points. Minutes later, she was done with the food and rushed back to the room to change. She wondered why she was so excited about the meeting.

She put on her clothes and grabbed her car key. Two hours later, she killed the engine in front of the restaurant and stepped out. As she pushed the door open, her mouth hung open as she saw Thomas sitting. He looked so dashing in his gray suit.

"I am not late," she muttered to herself.

She walked slowly to the table with a light smile, "Hello, Mr. Thomas Johnson."

A bright smile appeared on his face, "The youngest CEO in the building."

"It's so good to see you again," she said.

Thomas shrugged, "We sit now as partners and not employer and employee."

Sam dragged a chair slowly and sat down; she stared into his eyes. She had always loved doing that. His eyes still had that loving stare which was always in contrast with his cold face.

"Can we order something?" Thomas asked.

"Sure," she said.

"You like Chinese dishes?" He asked.

"Yeah, I never liked it before. Not until I tasted it with a Chinese friend," she said.

"You have a boyfriend?" He asked.

She glared at him, "I never said so."

She wondered why he was interested in that. She just noticed that something had changed in him. He wasn't that cold son of a bitch she knew. He had this warm aura circling around him.

"Sam, I want to apologize about the way I treated you at the company. I really missed your services. You practically had the Midas touch."

"Woah, this feels like medicine after death. Why are you saying this now?"

Mr. Johnson cleared his throat and tilted forward, "I grew up in a world different than yours. A world which taught me how to be harsh. I never knew how to express love properly."

Sam smiled and shook her head, "I never wanted your love, and I wanted you to see me for who I was. I have brought contracts to that company, I have always been hardworking. But, what do I get, reprimands and queries for minor mistakes."

Mr. Johnson stared at the table and then lifted his gaze upwards, "I am sorry."

Sam gasped, that was the first time of hearing the almighty Thomas Johnson apologize.

"Samantha, I am really sorry. Truly, I was an asshole. You were right. Growing up in an orphanage changed my perspective of life. But, I am willing to correct it."

Samantha took a deep breath, "I have heard you Sir. Let's go back to what brought us here."

Mr. Johnson took a deep breath, "You haven't accepted my apology."

Sam raised her gaze, "I have, and I have heard you. I accept your apology. Why are you making me sound like a high school principal?"

He smiled, "Thank you very much."

He reached out for his case on the floor and placed it on the table. "There is this prototype for a rare infection and we are trying to market it."

He placed the file before her, and she browsed through the folder. "This is going to be hard. What kind of disease is it?"

"It is a rare infection but very delayed. And, we have a target to market it across a million people in the states."

Sam took a deep breath, "I am not going to lie, this is going to be tough. Real tough and I don't know…"

"I trust you, that's why I want you on this job. You get a million dollars once we reach our target and you will help us reach our target," he said.

Sam nodded, "I am not assuring you. But, I will try my very best."

Mr. Johnson nodded, "I trust you."

Sam shook hands with him, and their gazes lingered.

"I am starting to see you in a different light now," she said, and they stood.

"We will keep in touch," Mr. Johnson said.

Sam nodded, and they both stepped out together. Sam entered into her car and watched as he drove out of the restaurant. She took a deep breath and ignited the engine. As she started to drive, her phone beeped. She picked it up; it was an email from the tech device producing company.

She opened it, *Samantha; we regret to inform you that we have ceased manufacturing the devices because of the conspiracies on the ground. We have also withdrawn your rights to the products, and the necessary paper works will be sent to you.*

She slumped onto the car steering.

S am drove back home in pain and heartache. She had woken up an hour later with a severe headache. Her phone kept ringing; it was her team members calling. She was sure that they were calling in regards to the email. If her partnering company was refusing to do business with her, that meant there was no need to run the company again. She arrived home and sunk into the sofa.

Her phone kept ringing; she picked it up and stared at it. It was Marcus on the line. She wasn't in the mood to answer his calls. She just headed to her room and dozed off. She woke up feeling refreshed but empty. She had lost every desire to continue. Her company started well until this conspiracy theory came up. She moved to the kitchen and decided to make some fries, but she lost her appetite. She went back to the room and watched her phone ring until it went off.

The next day was Sunday, and she was still in bed. She remained there until noon. Some minutes after noon, she heard a knock. She didn't want to see anybody, so she remained in bed. The knock continued, and she had no choice but to drag herself off the bed. She dragged her feet to the door and unlocked it.

"Sam!" Becky said with tears in her eyes. "I thought you committed suicide. You look rough."

Sam just bent her neck and walked back inside, with Becky following her. Becky made her sit and rushed into the kitchen to make tea. She returned shortly with a cup of tea and four slices of bread.

"The whole team has been scared. We have been trying to reach you," she handed the cup of tea to Sam, but she refused to take it.

"Sam, you need to eat. You look like you escaped prison," Becky urged.

"The team should continue without me for now. I need to figure out my life right now."

"No, we can't leave you now," Becky pressed the cup against her lips. "Just take a sip and come back to life."

Sam pushed the cup slightly away from her lips, "I have fought very well, and spent sleepless nights to reach this position. Only to be thrown off balance like this?"

Becky nodded, "I understand what's happening right now."

Sam nodded, "I need rest, please."

"I'm not going to let you slip into depression and die."

Sam knew Becky wouldn't give up unless she took the tea. She took the cup from her and took a sip.

"Try more, Sam," Becky urged.

Sam took a longer sip and took a bite of the bread, "I cleared things with the tech company. I don't know why they had to chicken out of operations."

Becky shrugged, "You won't blame them, and they are scared."

"Once I'm done clearing the loan without any major product moving into the market, we will go broke. And, being broke is being out of business."

Becky shook her head, "That's not going to happen."

"That's the obvious truth. We have no investors to fall back on major shares. And, Mr. Johnson met me for a project."

Becky raised an eye, "He did?"

Sam nodded, "I will call him later and inform him that I can't take up such a risky project. Not at this sick mental state of mine."

Becky stared at her friend with sorry eyes; Sam had been through a lot these past few months. She held her hands, "We will get past this. Don't make any calls."

Sam nodded, "I will."

Becky got up, "You need to charge your phone. Maybe you might have an important call, okay?"

Sam got up, moved to the room, and returned with her phone. She handed it to Becky, "I need to go back to bed."

"No," Becky shook her head, "You need to shower, please."

Sam nodded and moved into the bathroom; she took off her clothes slowly and then stepped into the bathtub. As the cold water touched her body, she shivered and rested her head on the wall. She stayed in there for so long, wondering where she got it all wrong.

Becky sprung out of the kitchen where she was making dinner and rushed into the bathroom. She pushed the door open, scaring Sam, who was in deep thought.

Sam took a deep breath, "You scared me."

"Did I? You have been in here for the past hour."

"I'm stepping out now," Sam got out of the bathtub; she reached for her towel and draped it around her body.

"I'm making spaghetti for dinner. Just the way you love it."

"Thank you," Sam replied.

Some minutes later, Sam stepped out of the room and moved to where her phone was being charged. She unplugged it and switched it on. Immediately after it was done booting, a call came in. It was from her tech guy.

"I have been trying to reach you, Ma'am."

"What is it?" she asked.

"I tracked the IP address to a certain Frank Mitchell. I've sent his picture to your email. He is the one responsible for the posts."

A ray of hope shimmered through her, and she smiled. "Thank you very much."

She knew she had heard the name before. She opened her email and browsed through it, she saw the pictures, and she quickly identified the dude. He was the executive assistant at Mines and Crafts. She nodded; she was going to fight him with every drop of blood in her body.

"Becky, Becky!"

She rushed out of the kitchen, "Any problem?"

"I've discovered who is behind the posts. We are paying him a visit tomorrow. Place a conference call, I need to speak with the team," Sam said with renewed hope.

Becky smiled, "I told you that we are going to get to the root of this. Let's go get that son of a bitch."

CHAPTER 17

Monday morning greeted Samantha with much enthusiasm. She wore a black cooperate top over a dark polka skirt. She slid dark sun-glasses over her face and marched to her car. She waited patiently for Becky to arrive with the security detail. Together, they made their way to *Mines and Crafts.*

They killed the engine, and they stepped out. The chief security guard approached the receptionist.

"We are looking for Frank Mitchell," the man barked.

The female receptionist's skin crawled in fear as she stared at the size of the man and the impact of his voice.

"He is in his office but I don't think he would stay for long," the lady replied.

"Take us to him," the security barked.

The receptionist led them to the office and pointed at the door. Samantha pushed it open, and they stepped inside. Frank's heart skipped a bit as he saw the people in his office.

"Frank Mitchell, why?" Sam asked.

Frank got up slowly, "I don't understand."

"The posts, the pictures. You think I won't find out?"

Frank shook his head, "I don't know what you are talking about."

The guard stepped forward, grabbed Frank's wrist and twisted it. Before Frank could scream, the guard shoved a piece of cloth in his mouth which shuffled his screams.

"You know; I remember when you came to my office. You sounded very cocky and I felt you had something sinister in mind. Do you know how much you have cost me?" Sam asked.

Frank still kept whimpering; he was in pain.

"I am going to ask you one last time, why?" Sam asked.

The guard pulled the cloth from his mouth, and Frank spat out spittle.

"You just trespassed, you are trampling on my right," Frank said. "I don't have any idea what you are talking about."

"You, son of a bitch. You think I don't have proof? I called your friend, the doctor yesterday, he identified you. I made a call to your

Boss and threatened to sue his firm for defamation for fifty million dollars, he told me everything. I came prepared."

Frank's breathing became labored, "I did it out of jealousy and resentment."

Sam laughed, "Jealousy, have I ever crossed path with you?"

"Not that. At your age, I tried starting my own business but I couldn't make it. I ran into debt and it ran into the ground. Seeing you do it effortlessly made me jealous."

Sam laughed, "Do you know how many sleepless nights went into developing the plan? Do you know how long I toured around the whole of this country searching for answers? Do you know how my eyes hurt, burning at night from staring at my laptop screen non-stop? No investor was willing to believe in me, not one. You came that day and acted like a cocky bastard."

Becky tapped at the bodyguard, "Give him a punch."

"No," Sam stepped forward, "I am going to be calling the press and you will have to personally debunked everything you said, and then I am out of here. If you don't, you are going to pay for defamation."

Frank nodded, "I will do that." He stared at Samantha; there was something so unique about her. She was strong; he could attest to that. And, she had a good spirit.

The guard led him out of the office, and they stepped outside.

In about thirty minutes, the press arrived. Frank got up and faced the camera.

"My name is Frank Mitchell and I have failed the city."

**

"I was wrong about the tech device. I acted impulsively without making my findings. I allowed myself to…" He cleared his throat, "I am not doing this under duress. I am putting this out because I am wrong. I apologize sincerely to Williams Ventures and everybody affected by my post. I will take them down. Finally, I am the man behind the anonymous post."

Sam picked up her phone and dialed her tech company. "Have you seen the press conference?"

"Yeah, that's a good thing. We will give you a reply before the end of the day."

Sam nodded and brought down her phone. She moved over to Frank, "If anything like this comes up in the future, I will sue you for defamation."

"I won't be coming to the firm today. I just want to be alone and go over some things. Hopefully, I will be back tomorrow," Sam said.

"Are you okay? Becky asked. "We are supposed to make that dude pay for all the pain he is causing you."

Sam chuckled, "I have him in my palms now. If the tech biz works out, they will be my first investor."

Becky nodded and hugged Sam, "I love you."

"Take care of the company," Sam replied.

"You know I will," Becky replied.

Sam nodded and got into her car and headed home. Her phone rang, and it was Marcus on the line; she wasn't in the mood to speak to anyone. She drove home, went into her room, and jumped into bed. She slept for hours and then woke up at dusk. She reached for her phone and dialed Marcus' number.

"Hey Marcus," she said.

"I thought you didn't want to talk to me again. And then, I saw the news. You are a strong woman."

She rolled her eyes, "Strong? I have heard that word several times today, please."

"I am heading back to China. I need to start up my company there. Europe has seen enough of me."

She wanted to flare up why she was hearing it now, but she remembered that she hadn't been picking up anyone's calls since the last weekend.

"Are you there?" He asked.

"Yes, I will miss you," she said.

"I would have asked you to come with me. But, your future is here."

She sniffed, "Thanks Marcus for everything."

"You have been a good student, Sam. I am proud to have you as a friend."

"Farewell, Marcus."

"Stay strong Samantha Williams. You are getting there," he said.

CHAPTER 18

It drizzled last night, and Samantha woke up to a text message. She picked up her phone and stared at it; her tech company was resuming production. She jumped out of the bed in excitement. She saw a notification of a missed call; it was from Thomas Johnson.

She decided to dial his number, and she waited patiently for it to ring. Her heart skipped as the call was answered.

"Hey, Sam."

He called her Sam, and she smiled.

"Hey, Boss," she whispered.

"Congratulations. I saw the press conference yesterday; you are breaking records. It isn't easy to have an adversary humbled to that extent. Maybe you are going to share some of your strategies with me."

She laughed, "I was almost at the verge of losing my mind."

"Yeah, it happens. So, have you started something on the project?" He asked.

"I will meet with my team today and we will look into it," Sam replied.

"Can we have dinner today?" He requested.

"Dinner?" She asked.

"Yeah, dinner," he replied.

"Like a date?" She asked further.

"Something like that," he replied.

She took a deep and thoughtful breath, "I…"

"You can refuse it if it doesn't favor you."

"No, I am fine. We are fine, just text me the address," she said.

"Okay, have a nice day, CEO," he greeted.

"You too," she greeted.

She threw the phone on the bed and danced into the bathroom. She stepped out an hour later and wore her clothes. She grabbed her car key and started to step out, but her phone beeped. She stared at the screen; it was a strange caller.

"Samantha Williams on the line."

"Frank Mitchell."

"Yes, Mr. Mitchell," she answered.

"As a sign of goodwill, my company would be investing in your real estate. We have sent some documents to your email."

Sam smiled, "Thank you very much. I will check on it."

"Hmm…I was wondering if I can have the chance to apologize properly during dinner."

Sam shook her head, "No, no. I am fine."

"Please, you won't regret it."

"I never said I would. See, I want us to have a professional relationship, okay?"

"Okay Miss Williams. Thank you."

Sam ended the call; why *is he thanking me? He is lucky I choose not to throw his ass into jail.*

She stepped out of the house and entered into her car. She drove to the firm and stepped out. All her team members stepped out and hugged her.

"I have great news," Sam said.

"I can't wait to hear it," Becky and Tara squealed.

"I will share it in the board room, okay?"

An hour later, everyone gathered in the board room. Sam cleared her throat and got up.

"I am sorry for shutting you guys out during the weekend. I was going through a whole lot and I needed to think about the way forward. I believe you all saw the email on Saturday. We were almost about to be thrown out of business. But then, there was a turn around. Right now, we have an investor and Mr. Thomas Johnson reached out to me for a project and we have to actualize as everyone here will be getting two hundred thousand dollars."

The next three hours were a brainstorming session in which everyone gave their ideas. Sam, with her wealth of knowledge and expertise, was able to narrow down the strategies to the necessary ones which were needed. By noon, the meeting ended, and they stepped out of the board room for lunch.

"Thomas asked me out for dinner," Sam whispered.

Becky turned to her, "You are just lucky. What magic do you perform on these guys?"

Sam shrugged, "I don't know."

Three hours later, Sam was home. She had her shower and settled for a red dinner gown and gladiator sandals. Thomas had sent the address of the restaurant. She entered into her car in a bid to reach the place early enough. She arrived after fifteen minutes and saw Thomas already. He was sipping from a glass of wine.

Thomas saw the angelic beauty before him, those hazel eyes. He had missed them; he got up and shifted a chair for her to sit. Sam was stunned at his romantic gesture. She sat on the chair with a bright smile; Thomas was looking dashingly handsome in his red suit. It seemed they picked the same color.

"You are looking very beautiful tonight," he complimented.

Sam nodded, "You aren't looking too bad yourself."

They placed their orders and started eating.

"Sam, how is your love life?" He asked.

She shrugged, "I haven't had time to think of that. It has been work and more work."

Thomas nodded, "I don't know how I am going to say it."

Sam's heart skipped, "What do you want to say?"

"I love you, Sam. I have been meaning to say it since the first day we started working together. I never knew how to say it and it kept frustrating me and I ended up pumping the frustration towards you."

Sam breathed, "I am listening, go on."

"How about we become close friends and see where this would lead us too. I don't want us to be in a rush."

Sam nodded, "So, friends we are right?"

Thomas nodded, "Close friends for now. But, I don't intend to be in that zone for too long."

"And what makes you think that I will be eager to leave the zone, I mean the friend zone."

Thomas nodded and stared into her eyes, "That is why I want to prove myself to you. I want to show you that I can be different. Different from the sadistic Boss you knew me for."

Sam nodded with a shrug, "Let us see how it goes."

They stared at each other and then looked away. Sam looked at his eyes; she had always loved those eyes. They kept on staring, breaking off their gaze.

"I love you Thomas and I hope we can work this out," she replied with a shrug.

Thomas smiled, "I hope we do."

A Year Later

"We did it," Sam screamed, "The numbers don't lie."

"Yes, we did it," Emily screamed, "We tripled the target."

Tara turned and hugged Sam, "Boss, I am proud of you."

"We did it together," Sam said.

"No, we wouldn't have done this without you. Your coaching and advise brought us this far. We almost gave up at some point," Becky said.

They were in the board room, and they had just made a total of three hundred million dollars from the sales of the rare drug, which was Thomas Johnson's project.

"I can't wait to break the news," Sam picked up her phone and raced out of the board room, she scrolled through her contacts to call Thomas. After a couple of short rings, Thomas answers, "Hello, darling."

"Hey, dear," Sam muttered excitedly.

"Hey, what is it? You sound so excited?"

"We tripled the target. I never wanted to monitor the numbers because it looked like we were not making headway. But, in the space of four months, we were able to penetrate the market. And now, the product has gone global."

"Damn babe, you are too intelligent. I am proud of you and I am happy. Remember you wanted to give up?"

She shrugged, "I didn't because I have a supportive boyfriend and an amazing team."

"Just hang on there for me, I am heading to your firm now," Thomas said.

"No, I can send the reports to you. You don't have to bother," she said.

"No, baby, I am coming for something worth more than the millions."

She chuckled; what *could it be?*

"You are an inspiration to all of us, Sam," Emily walked over to her.

Sam nodded, "I am glad."

Twenty minutes later, Thomas arrived at the firm. He stood in the hallway and blew a whistle. Everyone stepped down only to see him on his knees with a shiny box in his hands.

"I have watched you Sam. I watched as you grew from an intern to one of my most brilliant employee. From that, you started your own firm and in the space of months, you got over seventy investors. That is growth and I am proud to be part of it, I will ask you now, will you marry me?"

Sam squealed in excitement and stuck her finger forward, "Yes. I will. I will."

Everyone screamed in happiness.

Sam's journey serves as an inspiration for others, showing the importance of perseverance, taking control of one's life, and finding love in unexpected places.

The End

About the Author

J. D. Hova is an author who perfectly blends passion, hope, and real-life meanings in his romance books. When he is not writing, you can find him enjoying the great outdoors with his family, dogs, chickens, and new-born baby. J. D. believes that true love and happiness take time and his books reflect that belief. His stories capture the essence of life and offer a glimmer of hope through happy ever afters. If you enjoyed reading his books, please leave a review as he truly appreciates your feedback.

Acknowledgments

I want to take a moment to express my sincerest gratitude to all the amazing people in my life. Without the love and support of my readers, family, friends, and colleagues, I wouldn't be where I am today. I am so grateful for each and every one of you who has helped me along my path to happiness and success. I also want to give a special shoutout to those who hold me accountable and contribute so much to making this journey through life possible. And of course, I can't forget to thank the most important women who inspire me – Linda V., my sweet baby girl Ayla, Grandmother Louise, Mother Kathy, Sister Shannon and Aunt Christine. Thank you all from the bottom of my heart.